Hexagonal Architecture Explained

How the Ports & Adapters architecture simplifies your life, and how to implement it

Updated 1st Edition

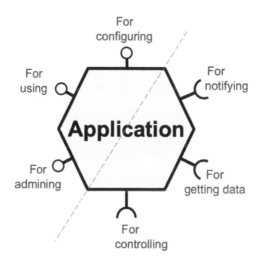

Alistair Cockburn

Juan Manuel Garrido de Paz

.

©Alistair Cockburn 2025 all rights reserved
ISBN 979-8-9985862-0-0 for paperback
ISBN 979-8-9985862-1-7 for ePub
Humans and Technology Press
5325 20th Ave S
Gulfport, FL 33707
v1.1b 20250420-1012 for paper&ePub books

Other books by Alistair Cockburn

1997 *Surviving Object Oriented Projects*
https://www.amazon.com/Surviving-Object-Oriented-Projects-Alistair-Cockburn/dp/0201498340

2000 *Writing Effective Use Cases*
https://www.amazon.com/Writing-Effective-Cases-Alistair-Cockburn/dp/0201702258

2001 *Agile Software Development (1st ed)*
https://www.amazon.com/Agile-Software-Development-Alistair-Cockburn/dp/0201699699

2002 *Patterns for Effective Use Cases*
https://www.amazon.com/Patterns-Effective-Cases-Software-Development/dp/0201721848

2003 *People and Methodologies in Software Development (Dr. Philos.)*
https://web.archive.org/web/20140329203845/http://alistair.cockburn.us/People+and+methodologies+in+software+development

2004 *Crystal Clear: A human-powered methodology for small teams*
https://www.amazon.com/Crystal-Clear-Human-Powered-Methodology-Development-ebook/dp/B00B8UX6K2

2006 *Agile Software Development: The cooperative game (2nd ed)*
https://www.amazon.com/Agile-Software-Development-Cooperative-Game-ebook/dp/B0027976NG

2021 *Design in Object Technology: Class of 1994*
https://www.amazon.com/Design-Object-Technology-Class-Object-Oriented-ebook/dp/B09GPP9K1L

2022 *Design in Object Technology: The Annotated Class of 1994*
https://www.amazon.com/Design-Object-Technology-Annotated-Class-ebook/dp/B0BFJYTRFP

2022 *Love Trio Trio del Amor (selected poems)*
https://www.amazon.com/Love-Trio-Amor-Alistair-Cockburn-ebook/dp/B0BPCCHZCG

2024 *Unifying User Stories, Use Cases, Story Maps (preview ed.)*
https://www.amazon.com/Unifying-User-Stories-Cases-Story-ebook/dp/B0D4JSQ5DY
ePub directly: https://store7710079.company.site/Unifying-User-Stories-Use-Cases-Story-Maps-epub-p655931612

2024 *Hexagonal Architecture Explained (preview ed)*
https://www.amazon.com/Hexagonal-Architecture-Explained-Alistair-Cockburn/dp/173751978X

2025 *Hexagonal Architecture Explained, Updated 1st ed.*
ePub directly: https://store7710079.company.site/Hexagonal-Architecture-Explained-ePub-p655931616

Kudos for the book

I just wanted to say thank you for hexagonal architecture.

My team used to do it for a while and we finally we got it right. Making changes to the services we hexagonalized properly feels really good and easy.The same changes kept giving us headaches in other services.

Your recent book recently helped us to gain confidence that we are doing it right and to see where ideas from other patterns were mixed in by people blogging on the topic.

Michael Kutz
Software Engineer at REWE digital GmbH

* * * * *

The publication of this book has been a great joy for several reasons. One of them is personal, as you might have guessed if you follow this blog. The other reason is that we finally have an authoritative reference guide to the pattern.

it is a very complete and detailed work. You can consider it a must-have reference both theoretically and practically, as it offers a fairly comprehensive implementation guide.

If you're really interested in understanding it and, possibly, using it in your projects, the book is the best source available, and it also includes the few original references you could find online.

Fran Iglesias,
Staff Software Engineer at Qualifyze

* * * * *

Been deep in Hexagonal Architecture lately—pure gold from @TotherAlistair & Juan Manuel Garrido de Paz. Highly recommend (get the book!)

Eugene F. Barker

* * * * *

I found the book to be very simple and practical. In fact, I used a few of its ideas in some refactoring I'm doing at work and they made a real difference.

What's more, it contains some detailed DDD discussion and its relation to Ports and Adapters!

Rubyists might be especially pleased to find examples of how to implement that architecture in Ruby (I definitely was!).
I strongly recommend it.

Hemal Varambhia
Senior Technical Coach

* * * * *

About the preview edition:

"It gives interesting insights not just on how the pattern can be implemented, but also on its story and the design considerations that revolve around it."

About the additions in the updated 1st edition:

"I find that the additions you did are very valuable not just in terms of understanding the pattern, but also in terms of understanding how it fits with the existing literature, related patterns, testing strategies etc."

Eleonora Ciceri

Acknowledgements

From Alistair

I am immensely grateful to Juan Manuel Garrido de Paz, without whom this book could never have been written. Of all the people I have conversed with, Juan had the sharpest, deepest, most accurate understanding of the pattern. He saw its relationship to UML components and the *required* interface years before I did.

He was relentless in his quest to understand and describe the pattern. He provided code for me to study and include. We argued incessantly, but only ever in pursuit of the truth. Once we found it, we were once again in complete agreement.

Juan was also a relentless fan of FC Huelva:

Juan at Huelva, 2024

I often think of the following, which he expressed to me during our work together. It serves to show both his personality, his dedication, and his wish to honor his father:

> *Lot of things left to do... I don't know if I will end it all for your conference. This is just a hobby for me. if you cannot reference my material, either because you don't like it, or because I don't finish it on time... it doesn't matter.*

I will keep on working on it anyway... My goal isn't to be "known" for this, my goal is just to learn and share my knowledge and try to explain correctly your pattern.

I'm honoured just because you consider my work, since I always try to be faithful to you, the original.

When I work I just think in my father, and in that my disease let me work on things that I like, like this, during the most possible time in the future.

I will always be thankful to you.
Juan.

From Juan
To my father

Four years before the hardest days of the COVID-19 pandemic, I was preparing a medium-large sized application for a nephew of mine, Emilio García Garrido, SEO consultant. It was a collaborative task management tool to be used by the members of a team. The app had 3-4 subsystems (yes, I know I'm old fashioned using that term instead of BC from DDD).

One day, looking at the screen of my laptop, I realized that it was full of framework code that didn't let me understand what it did regarding business logic. From that moment I began to search the internet and I discovered the architecture that decouples the business logic from the frameworks, and then I also heard of DDD.

From these architectures, the one I liked the most was Hexagonal Architecture, because the mechanism of ports-adapters to communicate is more flexible. That's how I discovered HA. From that moment on until nowadays (and i hope that in the future too) I haven't stopped reading and learning about this pattern.

Table of Contents

Preface

This is the full 1st edition

In early 2024, after working on this book for nearly 5 years, Juan and I (Alistair) felt the pressure to get it out "Now!". We decided to publish a *preview edition*, containing all the critical information, but possibly not in the best order, or needing better explanations in places.

That decision turned out to be prescient. Juan passed away very suddenly, just three weeks before the book was set to go to production. The preview edition came out barely in time for Alistair's visit to his home town, Sevilla, an emotional event, for sure. Happily, the book contains Juan's best thoughts up to that time.

Since then, I have watched numerous discussions online, I have taught to the book, found a few more topics for the FAQ section, and found one – almost humerously wrong – error in the first code sample. It is a credit to Juan that we argued so ferociously over the content that the content itself remains stable.

There are no significant changes to the original version, mostly I added a few pages of extra notes and fixed minor mistakes. The new text is marked with this solid gray bar down the side.

Since this update is from me alone, I will freely use the word 'I' and will feel free to add small anecdotes to make your reading a little more fun.

Alistair, April 10, 2025

(Preface to the *Preview* edition)

Juan and I feel it important enough to get this into your hands that we are publishing this edition before what normally constitutes fine tuning the book: sending to reviewers incorporating their changes, creating an index of key words, tuning page layout and so on. That process would take up to another year, and we feel you need this information today.

This edition has all the information we have at hand as of April 2024, in the best order we can think of. In other words, you can use it. Following this edition, I, Alistair, will continue to collect feedback and develop an improved 1st edition, which I may complete in 2025.

In the meantime, please enjoy this preview edition. Learn from it, practice it, and let me (totheralistair@aol.com) know your thoughts. Feedback on where you found things confusing, if something would be better in a different place, or where you might have misunderstood, will all help me develop a more accurate and comprehensive 1st edition.

How to read this book

Chapter 1: Introduction presents a small piece of sample code that illustrates the pattern, a brief timeline of the pattern, and the costs and benefits associated with it. We recommend you simply copy and paste the sample code into your system to give yourself a running start.

Chapter 2: Ports & Adapters Defined explains the pattern. It includes a definition of terms, and explores the four elements of the pattern as well as the configurator, which is not specified by the pattern but is still essential to understand. Chapter 2 also defines what is actually required and specified by the pattern, what is optional, and useful tips that are outside the pattern but may help in implementing it.

Chapter 3: Code Samples contains a series of code examples in several languages. They range from drop-dead simple to a fairly substantial app (which we still kept simple for readability). By exploring these samples, you can better see how the pattern functions in different, real-world environments.

Chapter 4: FAQ – What and How, and Chapter 5: FAQ – Related Concepts, contain our answers to Frequently Asked Questions, including handy metaphors and use cases for the pattern.

Chapter 6: The Original Articles covers the history of the pattern's genesis and evolution. It presents in full the original three articles that form the basis for how we talk about the pattern today.

Chapter 7: Summary is a synopsis of the book. It includes the pattern definition in short form, and repeats the code samples, cost, and benefits.

For your reading, we propose that you read Chapters 1 and 2 carefully, as they contain the best short description of the pattern at this time. If you are a programmer and like to dig through code, then Chapter 3 will show you how we implemented it ourselves. For the FAQ chapters, simply pick the topic or question that interests you and follow your nose. Finally, we include the original three articles so that you can see how much and how little has changed since 2005. And of course, flip back and forth to double-check your understanding.

> *Postscript: Juan Manuel Garrido de Paz passed away unexpectedly in April, 2024. I, Alistair, am simply taking to completion what we had already written. We were within two weeks of locking the text at the time of Juan's passing, and as such I am happy that this book shows all of his thinking and influence up to his last moments.*

Alistair, signing also for Juan,
April 23, 2024

Chapter 1:
Introduction

1.1. Copy this code

The Ports & Adapters architecture, first documented in 2005 as the "Hexagonal Architecture" pattern, demands this:

Create your application to work without either a UI or a database so you can run automated regression-tests against it, change connected technologies, protect it from leaks between business logic and technologies, work when the database becomes unavailable, and link applications together without any user involvement.

The most surprising part of implementing it is this requirement:

"Never explicitly name any external object or technology. Always take a parameter for any external object or technology you wish to access."

That requirement has a weak and a strong implementation. In the "weak" implementation, the programmer knows that the database will use SQL (for example), and without tying to a particular database, still expresses the interface in SQL. While technically meeting the rules of the Ports & Adapters architecture, that still handcuffs the system to SQL, which is not what we are after.

To get a full, or "strong" implementation of the Ports & Adapters architecture, we need:

"The app cannot know anything about the external technology."

That is, the Service Provider Interface (SPI) or "driven port" is expressed purely in terms of concepts that make sense in the language of the domain. It can't even know that there is a database, let alone SQL.

The easiest way to show this is with a bit of code. The code is much simpler than all the discussions of why the code looks that way.

Therefore, to get started, replicate this code snippet in your larger system. This Java code shows the interface definitions explicitly:

```java
interface ForCalculatingTaxes {
   double taxOn(double amount);
}
```

```java
interface ForGettingTaxRates {
   double taxRate(double amount);
}
```

```java
class TaxCalculator implements ForCalculatingTaxes {
   private ForGettingTaxRates taxRateRepository;
   public TaxCalculator(ForGettingTaxRates taxRateRepository) {
      this.taxRateRepository = taxRateRepository;
   }
   public double taxOn(double amount) {
      return amount *  taxRateRepository. taxRate( amount );
   }
}
```

```java
class FixedTaxRateRepository
      implements ForGettingTaxRates {
   public double taxRate(double amount) {
      return 0.15;
   }
}
```

```java
class Main {
   public static void main(String[] args) {
      ForGettingTaxRates taxRateRepository = new
                                    FixedTaxRateRepository();
      ForCalculatingTaxes myCalculator = new TaxCalculator(
                                    taxRateRepository );
      System.out.println( myCalculator.taxOn( 100 ) );
   }
}
```

The preview edition contained a mistake. Without studying the previous code, see if you can find it in this original version:

```
interface ForCalculatingTaxes {
   double taxOn(double amount);
}
```

```
interface ForGettingTaxRates {
   double taxRate(double amount);
}
```

```
class TaxCalculator implements ForCalculatingTaxes {
   private ForGettingTaxRates taxRateRepository;
   public TaxCalculator(ForGettingTaxRates taxRateRepository) {
      this.taxRateRepository = taxRateRepository;
   }
   public double taxOn(double amount) {
      return amount * taxRateRepository. taxRate( amount );
   }
}
```

```
class FixedTaxRateRepository
      implements ForGettingTaxRates {
   public double taxRate(double amount) {
      return 0.15;
   }
}
```

```
class Main {
   public static void main(String[] args) {
      ForGettingTaxRates taxRateRepository = new
                                  FixedTaxRateRepository();
      TaxCalculator myCalculator = new TaxCalculator(
                                  taxRateRepository );
      System.out.println( myCalculator.taxOn( 100 ) );
   }
```

I could say, "almost comical," because Ricardo Guzmán Velasco (@RGVgamedev on Twitter) found it at the book launch. He came up and said he didn't understand why I needed the driving port declaration. I went to explain, pulled my finger down the code, and went, "Crap." He found the mistake within minutes of launch. Sigh.

The mistake is giving myCalculator type TaxCalculator, that is, typing with the class instead of the interface. With that mistake, the interface definition at the top is meaningless.

What followed over the next months was interesting. Some people wrote in and said that the interface declaration was important:

* Convention: It is the standard programming convention in languages that have that feature to type by interface, not class.

* The interface declaration is intended to provide the minimum interface that we want to expose.

* If every client couples to TaxCalculator, you lose the freedom to change its implementation. If you create another ForCalculatingTaxes implementation, you have to change all clients when you want to switch the implementation.

* The purpose of type-checking is to catch a certain class of errors at compile time. Declaring the type as the class and not the interface defeats the purpose of typing. You lose the safety you thought you were getting.

Others wrote to say that there is no real problem in typing the variable with the class because for an app, the public methods are probably exactly the interface it should export, and you're unlikely to make a second implementation of the app. Shoutout to Nicky Ramone (@nickyramone77) and Chris F Carroll (@chrisfcarroll.bsky.social) for these insights.

For them, the interface declaration at the top is unnecessary, which means the published code is still not right.

In the end, it seems there are two reasonable schools of thought, each with its own defenders.

In one, declare and use the interface declaration:

```
interface ForCalculatingTaxes {
    double taxOn(double amount);
}
```

```
class TaxCalculator implements ForCalculatingTaxes {
    ... (public methods) ...
}
```

```
class Main {
    ...
    ForCalculatingTaxes myCalculator = new TaxCalculator(
                                    taxRateRepository );
}
```

In the other, don't declare it. Just use the class:

```
interface ForCalculatingTaxes {
    double taxOn(double amount);
}          (don't write this code)
```

```
class TaxCalculator {
    ... (public methods) ...
}
```

```
class Main {
    ...
    TaxCalculator myCalculator = new TaxCalculator(
                                    taxRateRepository );
}
```

My mistake was having a foot in each camp, declaring the interface and then not using it.

In your life, decide which way you prefer to write.

Not all languages require type declarations. In these languages, the code is much simpler. The following Ruby code shows how dynamic languages create the same system with no interface definitions:

```ruby
class TaxCalculator
  def initialize( tax_rate_repository )
    @tax_rate_repository = tax_rate_repository
  end

  def tax_rate( amount )
    @tax_rate_repository.tax_rate( amount )
  end

  def tax_on( amount )
    amount * @tax_rate_repository.tax_rate( amount )
  end
end
```

```ruby
class FixedTaxRateRepository
  def tax_rate( amount )
    0.15
  end
end
```

```ruby
tax_rate_repository = FixedTaxRateRepository.new
my_calculator = TaxCalculator.new( tax_rate_repository )
puts my_calculator.tax_rate( 100 )
puts my_calculator.tax_on( 100 )
```

It will take the rest of this book to explain how that little bit of code is constructed, why it is done that way, and how to make it work in your setting.

That doesn't mean you should wait until you've read the whole book before getting started. We recommend you start now by copying that code into your workspace and building from there. We also recommend you read Chapter 4.8: Where do I put my files? if you have any questions about folder structures.

1.2. Short history of the pattern

1988: Alistair unknowingly implemented Model-View-Controller in his Smalltalk prototype, but his C programmer didn't. When the need arose to change the source of inputs, the C program had to be torn apart and rewritten. Pain #1.

1994: On a fixed-price, fixed-time project involving an object-relational mapper, the infrastructure designers found they had to change their design to the SQL database to improve performance. As the application programmers were unable to substitute an in-memory test database, they instead shut down the project for several weeks and frantically rewrote their mapper. Pain #2.

2000: Alistair visited a friend who was having trouble with all the variants and versions of his application, with different input sources and notification methods. Those problems were solved using the Ports & Adapters architecture.

2005: Alistair finally implemented the pattern on a real project (using Spring) and wrote it up with code samples, giving it the more accurate name, "Ports & Adapters."

2015: The notions of driving and driven adapters were added, along with the naming convention for interfaces as "for_doing_something."

2022: The pattern as a special case of "Component + Strategy" was formulated, along with the *required interfaces* concept.

2023: The more complete and accurate *Configurable Receiver* pattern replaced the earlier, slightly incorrect pattern "Configurable Dependency."

2024: Juan and Alistair complete their collaboration to bring you the preview edition of this book.

1.3. Why the name "Hexagonal" Architecture?

The name "Hexagonal Architecture" was a placeholder name I (Alistair) came up with years before I understood what the sides of the hexagon stood for. I just knew they had to be there. As a pattern name, it is not really appropriate, since the number six has no particular meaning. In practice you might have three, five, or any number of ports, not six. Additionally, a hexagon is just a geometric shape. It doesn't show up anywhere in your software.

So why the name, and why change it to the more descriptive *Ports & Adapters*?

The best answer is what I wrote in the RSS feed from 2005, when I finally worked out what the facets meant:

> *Somewhere in the mid-90s I started drawing a symmetric architecture in which the database is considered not at the "bottom of the stack", but fully outside the application, just as we recommend doing with the user interface.*
>
> *To break up perceptions about top and bottom and left and right, I drew it with a hexagonal shape, and came up with the rather lame name HexagonalArchitecture --- simply because I could not identify think of what the "hexagon" meant, but knew it had to have facets, and no number smaller than 5 made visual sense (and pentagons are harder to draw than hexagons).*
>
> *Finally just worked out what the drawing meant and realized this picture or architecture should be called Ports and Adapters (think operating system or hi-fi ports, and Design Pattern "adapters").*
> *-*
> *https://web.archive.org/web/20060318201137/http:/alistair.cockburn.us/rss.rdf (time stamp: 2005 07 15 13:01 MST)*

"Hexagonal Architecture" has served well as a hook to the pattern. It's easy to remember and generates conversation. However, in this book we want to be correct: The name of the pattern is "Ports & Adapters", because there really are ports, and there really are adapters, and your architecture will show them.

1.4. The costs and benefits of this pattern

There are many benefits to the Ports & Adapters, AKA Hexagonal Architecture, code structure:

1. Testing: You can write and run system-level tests without production connections, making them purer and faster.

2. More on testing: You can swap out the production connections for test connections, and vice versa—for any of the connections, input or output—without having to recompile your system.

3. Leakage protection: The test wall around your application will detect whenever someone leaks UI details or technology details into the business section, or business logic into the UI or external technology sections.

4. Large system separations: Different teams can develop their sections of code independently, test them separately, and connect them according to defined and tested interfaces.

5. Long-running systems: You can replace one external connection with another as technology and business needs change over a period of years.

6. Domain-Driven Design: Once the technology elements are safely outside the application boundary, you are free to focus on the domain design without distraction.

There is also a complexity cost to implementing this structure. You'll see this cost more for type-declared languages than dynamic or type-inferred languages.

1. You will either add an instance variable for each driven actor, or else get that information every time you need it.

2. You will either add a constructor parameter or a setter function for each driven actor, or else a call to the configurator to get that information.

3. You must design and add a configurator.

4. In type-declared languages, you must declare the *required* interfaces (see Chapter 2.2. *The Pattern Elements: Apps, Ports, Actors, Adapters.*

5. In type-declared languages, you will add additional folder structure for the port declarations.

You may ask, how should I balance the costs against the benefits?

People who have never been hurt by changing technology, shifting interfaces, business logic leaking out, external technology details leaking in, or having to recompile the system to switch between testing and production, say that the costs look too high to be worth implementing the pattern.

It seems to take people suffering on a project for them to decide that adding a few interfaces and instance variables is worth the trouble.

For the two of us, this is now our default way of building applications or systems. It would take special circumstances, like writing a one-off program, for us not to use it.

Chapter 2:
Ports & Adapters Defined

2.1. Glossary

We'll be using a number of terms throughout this book which we recommend you familiarize yourself with in advance.

Application: The software that we are putting a boundary around. It contains all the business logic, and no reference to technologies, databases, networks, humans, or code outside the scope of development. All technology is external to the application, including any adapters needed to translate to or from it.
Synonyms: App, Hexagon, System, SuD, SuT, Core.

Extended System: The wider system that includes adapters and immediately connected technology such as databases, repositories, network interfaces, GUI.

Actor: Anything with behavior, whether hardware, software, a person, or an organization. A thing has behavior if it is able to execute an "if" statement.

Primary or driving actor: An actor that will initiate a conversation with the app, will make a service request of the app, or will kick the app out of its quiescent state. *Primary* and *driving* are synonyms. It is possible for one actor to be primary in some situations and secondary in others.

Secondary or driven actor: An actor that the app will initiate a conversation with, will make a service request of, or will get kicked out of its quiescent state by the app. *Secondary* and *driven* are synonyms. It is possible for one actor to be primary in some situations and secondary in others.

Interactor: An interactor is that piece of software that interacts directly with the port. When a primary or secondary actor doesn't need an adapter to connect with a port, the interactor is that actor. When an actor needs an adapter to connect with a port, the interactor is the adapter and the actor is largely out of the conversation. "Interactor" is a synonym for "an actor or an adapter."

Interface: A set of method definitions declared by an actor, specifying a contract to be fulfilled by the one that realizes (implements) the interface.

Provided interface: An interface that defines the services offered by the app. It is used by driving interactors, and is realized (implemented) by the app. Also: API (Application Programming Interface).

Required interface: An interface that defines the services needed by the app to perform its function. It is used by the app, and is realized (implemented) by the driven interactors. In the case of dynamic languages, where interfaces are not declared, the required interface is just "all the calls the app will make" at that port. Also: SPI (Service Provider Interface).

Port: A provided or required interface defined by the app. A port captures the idea of a conversation created for some intention between an external actor and the app. The port's name describes that intention (e.g., "forPlacingOrders").

Primary or Driving Port: A port with one or more provided interfaces, used by driving interactors to make requests of the app. Also: Inbound port, API.

Secondary or Driven Port: A port with one or more required interfaces, used by the app to make requests of driven interactors. Also: Outbound port, SPI.

Adapter: Code needed to fit the app's interfaces to those of driving or driven actors. An adapter translates messages from technology-specific external actors into technology-neutral requests at a port, and vice versa.

Primary or Driving Adapter: An adapter connecting a driving actor to a driving port. Also: Inbound adapter, API adapter.

Secondary or Driven Adapter: An adapter connecting a driven actor to a driven port. Also: Outbound adapter, SPI adapter.

The difficulty of naming

We sweated over naming. The thing is, there are three things to talk about: actor, adapter, and port. We need two adjectives for each and tried all of these: driving/driven, inbound/outbound, primary/secondary, API/SPI, left/right.

In the preview edition we used driving/driven and primary/ secondary. Some people found these terms difficult to use, and wrote inbound/outbound or API/SPI instead.

Only *driving/driven* and *primary/secondary* apply to all three, actor, adapter and port. You can talk about a driving actor, a driving adapter, a driving port, and similarly for the driven side. You can also talk about a primary actor, a primary adapter, a primary port, and similar for secondary.

But you can't say "inbound actor" and "outbound actor." Similarly, "API actor", "SPI actor" make no sense.

Personally, I (Alistair) don't mind synonyms. If you like inbound/ outbound port, and inbound/outbound adapter, that's fine. For the ports, having "API ports" and "SPI ports" makes sense, since ports are just interfaces anyway.

Where you might find "inbound" and "outbound" most useful is in naming your folders. Alistair never liked seeing two folders next to each other called Driven Adapters and Driving Adapters. They are just too similar. Calling them Inbound Adapters and Outbound Adapters seems like a good idea. Alistair has also seen "Provided/Required" and "Controllers/Providers." (More on folder structure in Chapter 4.8: Where do I put my files?)

In this book we stick with driving/driven and primary/ secondary, so that we can apply the same adjective to actor, adapter and port. But in your life, feel free to use inbound /outbound for your ports and adapters, if you like, or API /SPI for your ports if that's all you're talking about.

2.2. The pattern elements: App, Ports, Actors, Adapters

The Ports & Adapters pattern calls for four basic elements. There is a fifth element that is officially outside the pattern, but which you will in fact need.

The four elements that are part of the pattern proper are

1. the application or system itself, which we will call the "app",

2. the ports,

3. the driving and driven external actors,

4. adapters as needed at each port.

Some code has to connect these four parts. That is the *configurator*. The configurator is, strictly speaking, outside the pattern. As such, we will discuss it separately.

1. The app or system

The *app* or the *system* is whatever business logic you need in order to provide your desired functions, up to but not including any external technology. The app is technology-agnostic. It is written only in terms of the business, without reference to any particular technology or platform connected to it.

The Ports & Adapters pattern has you identify the places where your application meets the outside world. "The outside world" is easy to identify: it will usually be a physical element such as a database, a human user, or a network link. You may also encounter situations where the outside world is a social boundary; that is, where your project team's influence ends. In such a case, you create a hard, technical boundary with declared interfaces and protocols, and of course, tests to protect that boundary.

In both cases, you have created a "component." As described in *Component + Strategy generalizes Ports & Adapters* (Chapter 6.4), a component declares two interfaces: the *provided interface*, and the *required interface.*

The *provided interface*, as it is called in the Unified Modeling Language (UML), is the set of services the app offers to the outside world.

The *required interface*, as it is called in UML, is what the system requires any other entity to provide to it as *their* provided interface.

The first interface, the provided interface, is what we expect from any application or system: an API or calling interface. It's the *required* interface that is more surprising, and what makes the Ports & Adapters pattern so powerful.

Thus, for all external entities, primary or secondary, the app says, "I will only talk to you if you talk in my language," and explicitly defines that language. This is what makes it a component, something you can pick up out of a catalog and place into any system. All its boundary protocols are completely defined.

Even if you never intend to put this app into a catalog or use it in a different context, by putting the hard boundary around our system, we gain the benefits we are after: testability, protecting the business logic from leaking out, and the ability to change external technologies.

2. The ports

The ports define the true boundary of the application.

Every interaction between the app and the outside world happens at a port interface, using the interface language the app itself defines. As such, the ports are the demarcation of what is *inside* the app proper, and what is *outside*.

We organize interactions between the application and the external actors by the reason why they are interacting with the application. In this model, each set of interactions with a given purpose or intention is a *port*.

Because the interactions are grouped by their intention, we like to name a port for that intention, written as: "For doing something." The name starts with the word "For", then a verb ending in -ing, then whatever else is needed to make the purpose clear. Some examples are:

"For managing the contents of the shopping cart"

"For configuring the system"

"For sending notifications"

With that naming, the app has no idea what technology is outside the port. It is isolated from the world, interacting only through its ports.

That allows ports to be configured at run time, and connected to whatever is needed at that time. It is this property that gives the pattern its power.

We often find three sorts of driving ports:

* For instantiating and configuring the system,

* For performing administrative work on the system,

* For using the system to get business work done.

We also see three general sorts of driven ports:

* For getting information from a repository,

* For notifying someone,

* For controlling some device.

In some programming languages, such as Java and C++, the port has to be declared explicitly. In others, such as Ruby and Python, ports are not explicitly declared and are therefore not explicitly visible in the code.

3. The external actors

The Ports & Adapters pattern is intentionally symmetric. It speaks only about what is *inside* the app versus *outside* the app, with the app's ports as its boundary definition.

In implementation, however, there is an important asymmetry, the matter of *who* knows about *whom* in order to make a function call.

The app doesn't have to know who is calling its provided interface. The calling object has to know about the function in the app. It has to have the app's identity or handle in order to make the service call.

The app does have to know the object it is calling through it's required interface, though. To make a service request of an external entity, the app must have the handle for that entity.

To help understand and define this difference, we use the terms *driving* actors (the ones that drive the app), and *driven* actors (the ones that are driven by the app).

It turns out that the world of use cases (see Chapter 5.1, *How does this relate to use cases?*) already has words that fit nicely here: *primary* and *secondary* actors.

A *primary* actor is any entity, whether human or electronic, that kicks the app into action. It makes a service request of the app, initiating what may be a complex set of back-and-forth interactions.

A *secondary* actor is any entity, human or electronic, that the app kicks into action, requesting a service from it.

These terms match perfectly with the idea of ports. Primary actors become driving actors, which interact at the *driving* or *primary* ports. Secondary actors become driven actors, which interact at the *driven* or *secondary* ports.

By borrowing from use case language, we now see how many ports to put into an app and how to segment our interfaces into ports: An actor in a use case is characterized by their reason for interacting with the system. This means that we start by making a port for every actor, and for each interface, we ask what actor it serves.

Over time you might decide to change or build upon that initial architecture, but at least you'll have a good starting point.

4. The adapters

It is possible that a driving or driven actor already knows and uses the provided or required interface. No adapter is needed in these cases. For example:

When starting to develop the system, you are likely to write test cases to drive the app. You may code the app's provided interface straight into the test cases, or create mock databases or test doubles on the driven side that respond directly to the app's required interface.

You may design two apps to work together from the beginning. Each is a ports-and-adapters structured app in its own right, but by design you make their interfaces match.

In cases like these, you do not need an adapter. The external actors already meet the provided and required interfaces.

In other situations, where an external actor doesn't match the app's interface, you have to write code to transform the one actor's interface into the other's. That code is an *adapter*.

You're already familiar with adapters. A human sitting at the computer can't directly call the app. Instead, they interact via some kind of user interface, whether a command line interface (CLI) or a voice or graphical user interface (GUI). These adapters convert human movements into the application's interface, allowing the app and the human to interact.

A CLI or GUI to a human might also be placed on the driven side. For example, while developing an artificial intelligence (AI) engine, you might use a person to provide the responses needed by the app.

Adapters are generally needed for any sort of real-world technology. This includes the internet, a database, a paging system, real-time feed, or as mentioned, a human.

Adapters exist outside the app. As such, how you organize your adapters is up to you. The Ports & Adapters pattern neither legislates how you organize the insides of your app nor how you organize the things outside the app. The Ports & Adapters architecture says only that there is an *inside* and an *outside,* and the boundary between the two is defined by the ports (provided and required).

That said, much confusion arises about how to organize the adapters. A badly organized adapter structure can easily confuse programmers regarding where to put their code and what is really happening during interactions between the inside and outside. For that reason, we will spend some time in this book discussing good ways to structure the adapter code.

2.3. The 5th element: The Configurator

Something has to connect all the pieces. Some piece of code somewhere has to tell the drivers how to reach the app and tell the app which driven actors to use. This is the role of the configurator.

To do its job, the configurator has to know all the players: the app, the driving actors or their adapters, and the driven actors or their adapters.

How you design the configurator is not specified by the pattern. There are many ways to design it, depending on your situation. However you arrange it, the following actions must take place:

1. Instantiate each driven interactor (a driven adapter or a driven actor that needs no adapter).

2. Instantiate the app.

3. Provide the app with those driven interactors.

Instantiate each driving Interactor (actor or adapter) and pass it the app to use.

There are three ways to get the app to know a driven actor:

*   The configurator passes the driven actor into the app's constructor.

*   The app offers a function in its provided interface for setting the driven actor. A driving actor calls that function to set the driven actor at any time.

*   The app uses a service locator and asks the service locator what driven actor to use.

You can use a dependency injection framework like Spring for either of the first two cases.

Figure 2.1 illustrates what steps the configurator would take in the first scenario, when all the connections are made at system initialization.

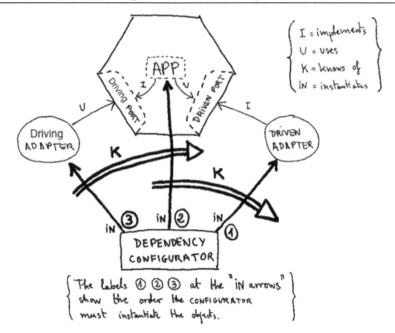

Figure 2.1. The configurator introduces the actors.

In this figure:

1. The configurator first instantiates all driven adapters (or gets the IDs of any driven actors which need no adapter).

2. It then instantiates the app and sets the driven actor(s) in the app's constructor.

3. Finally, it instantiates each driving adapter, passing the app to it.

In testing, the test cases act both as the configurator and the driving actor. It creates and connects the players as in Figure 2.1, and then drives the app.

In production, "main" or the composition root usually acts as the configurator and pulls all the players together.

2.4. What is required, optional, and outside the pattern

To apply a pattern, you need to know what is within the scope of the pattern itself, what is not part of the pattern but might be a useful tip, and what isn't part of the pattern at all.

What is required by the pattern

The pattern requires these things:

1. The app defines a provided or required interface for all external interactions.

2. The app defines driving ports for the provided interfaces and driven ports for the driven interfaces. In languages that don't require interfaces to be declared, these may not be explicitly visible.

3. The app allows the driven actors to be configured at run time.

4. The app has no source code dependencies on its primary or secondary actors.

5. External actors can interact only with the defined ports. They are not allowed to access anything inside the hexagon directly.

6. The ports and interfaces are not only technology-neutral, they use terms that only express business needs.

Useful tips, not required by the pattern

The pattern doesn't require these things, but implementing them will likely make your life easier:

1. The pattern says nothing about how you implement the configurator. You may find it useful to review the examples of configurators provided in this book.

2. The pattern does not legislate how you name your ports. Even so, we recommend the naming convention "For doing something", as it helps communicate why interfaces are bundled together.

3. The pattern says nothing about how granular the ports are, or how many functions are bundled into one port. In practice, we prefer fewer to more, starting with one port per primary actor

and one per secondary, as those match intentions for conversations.

4. The pattern says nothing at all about how you organize your codebase. We recommend the following to make it easy for people to read the code and retain the architecture:

    Make two port folders: "Driving Ports" and "Driven Ports." Place them alongside the app folder, as they are part of the app.

    Make two adapter folders, "Driving Adapters" and "Driven Adapters." Place them in a different space than the app folder.

5. The pattern says nothing about how you organize and design your adapters, including whether they ever interact directly or not. Aside from test cases, the driving adapters do not normally interact directly with the driven adapters. Of course, there may be exceptions that we haven't yet encountered.

6. The pattern does not specifically exclude the possibility that you have a Ports & Adapters subsystem inside some larger Ports & Adapters system.

    If we consider Ports & Adapters as a special case of Component + Strategy, this implies that the inner Ports & Adapters component will both be configurable to have different secondary actors, and will be completely tested in isolation from the rest of the larger Ports & Adapter system (see Chapter 6.4, *The Article: Component + Strategy generalizes Ports & Adapters*).

    While not impossible, this strikes us as unlikely. For this reason, we say that the pattern does not nest. See *What About Nested Hexagons?* (Chapter 5.8).

Not part of the pattern at all

The pattern has absolutely nothing to say about how you structure your application internally. You are welcome to use Domain Driven Design (DDD) or not; you are welcome to separate function from model, or not; you are welcome to make a big ball of mud, or not.

The pattern does not constrain your internal structuring philosophy. This makes it different from Clean and Onion architectures. See *Layered, Onion, Clean, Hexagonal: What is the Difference?* (Chapter 5.5).

Weak versus strong conformance to the pattern

You can implement this pattern in a legal but weak way. Suppose you know that the database will use SQL. Without tying to a particular database, you still express the driven port in SQL. While technically meeting the rules of the architecture, that still ties your system to SQL, which is not what we are after.

To get a proper, or strong implementation of the Ports & Adapters architecture,

> the app cannot know *anything* about the external technology.

That is, the driven port is expressed purely in terms of concepts that make sense in the application language. It can't even know that there a database, let alone an SQL one.

Chapter 3:
Code Samples

The best way to understand the pattern is to read and experiment with code in different languages and different environments. Here are four examples, working from the simplest to the most complex.

3.1. The simplest example: the tax calculator

You've already encountered our first and simplest code example back in Chapter 1.1. If you haven't already copied and pasted it, now's the time.

We chose a tax calculator because tax calculators can be as simple or complex as you need. We will start simple, with just one driving and one driven port. The driving port offers just the function *tax_on(amount)*.

We present this example in four parts:

1. First, we show just the *tax_on()* function in use. We use the simplest rate repository, which returns a fixed rate. This is the first step in creating architecture with as little code as possible.

   From this point forward, the drivers, port interfaces, business logic contained within the app and repositories can all change and grow, without any need to change the fundamental architecture.

   We use Java for this first part, because it helps show the ports being defined and used.

2. Second, the same code in Ruby. This illustrates how the code looks when it's not necessary to declare the ports or interfaces.

3. Third, using setter injection instead of dependency injection. The driven actor is not set in the constructor, but in a setter method. This allows the driven actor to be changed at any time.

4. Fourth, a different configurator, one that uses dependency lookup instead of dependency injection for the configurator.

   The tax calculator is augmented to hook to different rate repositories for different countries. The configurator is now a "rate repository broker" that says what rate repository to use for any country requested. This permits different tax tables for different countries, or for adapters to connect to the official tax authority for different countries.

   Of course, we need a second port for this broker, and therefore a test double for it, as well as a configurator for the broker.

The simplest tax calculator (Java)

In this simple example of the tax calculator, the configurator main() passes the receiver to the sender at object creation time. It creates the FixedTaxRateRepository, the receiver, and sends it to the TaxCalculator as part of its constructor.

For early development, I use an in-code tax rate repository with just one fixed tax rate. We chose to begin with Java, to show the interfaces.

```java
interface ForCalculatingTaxes {
    double taxOn(double amount);
}
```

```java
interface ForGettingTaxRates {
    double taxRate(double amount);
}
```

```java
class TaxCalculator implements ForCalculatingTaxes {
    private ForGettingTaxRates taxRateRepository;

    public TaxCalculator(ForGettingTaxRates taxRateRepository) {
        this.taxRateRepository = taxRateRepository;
    }

    public double taxOn(double amount) {
        return amount * taxRateRepository. taxRate( amount );
    }
}
```

```java
class FixedTaxRateRepository implements ForGettingTaxRates {
    public double taxRate(double amount) {
        return 0.15;
    }
}
```

```
class Main {
    public static void main(String[] args) {
        ForGettingTaxRates taxRateRepository = new
            FixedTaxRateRepository();
        ForCalculatingTaxes myCalculator = new TaxCalculator(
            taxRateRepository );
        System.out.println( myCalculator.taxOn( 100 ) );
    }
```

Notes:

"ForCalculatingTaxes" is the driving port, with, just for the moment, only one function offered: "taxOn(amount)."

"ForGettingTaxRates" is the driven port. It requires every repository to support the function "taxRate(amount)."

The TaxCalculator implements the driving port, and uses the driven port.

The FixedRateRepository implements the driven port, as every rate repository would do.

Main acts as both the configurator and, in this tiny case, also the driving actor. The first two lines act as the configurator, creating the FixedRateRepository and feeding it to the TaxCalculator at creation time. The last line is using the driving port as any user might.

The simplest tax calculator (Ruby)

This code accomplishes the same work as the prior Java example, but in Ruby. The ports and interfaces don't have to be declared in Ruby, which makes it difficult to see where they are.

```ruby
class TaxCalculator

  def initialize( tax_rate_repository )
    @tax_rate_repository = tax_rate_repository
  end

  def tax_on( amount )
    amount * @tax_rate_repository.tax_rate( amount )
  end
end
```

```ruby
class FixedTaxRateRepository
  def tax_rate( amount )
    0.15
  end
end
```

```ruby
tax_rate_repository = FixedTaxRateRepository.new
my_calculator = TaxCalculator.new( tax_rate_repository )
puts my_calculator.tax_rate( 100 )
```

Using a setter instead of constructor argument (Java)

In this example, we build upon previous examples to show that one doesn't have to set the driven actors in the constructor arguments (constructor injection). It is just as valid to use a setter method (setter injection). This allows the driven actors to be changed at any time.

Using setter injection instead of constructor injection comes with one hazard, namely that it is possible to construct the app and never actually set the driven actors, which leaves the app in an inconsistent state.

For long-running systems, setter injection is necessary, so the tests have to mitigate that hazard. Neither Juan nor Alistair has experience with these systems, so we can't comment further.

Here is the example of using setter injection:

```java
interface ForGettingTaxRates {
    double taxRate(double amount);
}
```

```java
class TaxCalculator {
    private ForGettingTaxRates taxRateRepository;

    public void setTaxRateRepository(ForGettingTaxRates
            taxRateRepository) {
      this.taxRateRepository = taxRateRepository;
    }
    public double taxOn(double amount) {
      return amount * taxRateRepository.taxRate( amount );
    }
}
```

```java
class FixedTaxRateRepository implements ForGettingTaxRates {
    public double taxRate(double amount) {
        return 0.15;
    }
}
```

```java
class Main {
    public static void main(String[] args) {
      ForGettingTaxRates taxRateRepository = new
          FixedTaxRateRepository();
```

```
      TaxCalculator myCalculator = new TaxCalculator();
      myCalculator.setTaxRateRepository( taxRateRepository );
      System.out.println(myCalculator.taxOn( 2000 ));
   }
}
```

Using a broker instead of a fixed rate repository (Ruby)

The fourth adjustment shows the use of *dependency lookup* instead of *configurable receiver* to configure the driven actor.

We introduce a rate repository broker, which will tell the calculator what rate repository to use for any given country. This allows different rate repositories to handle the different tax rate tables in various countries, or to have an adapter that connects directly to a country's official tax authority.

To do this, we introduce another driven port, "ForGettingCountryBasedTaxRateRepository." This port requires one function, RepositoryForCountry(country).

Now that we have a second port, we need to be able to test it. There needs to be a test double as well as a production rate repository broker. This in turn means we need a configurator for the broker port. Here we use constructor injection to set the broker to use at the time the tax calculator is created.

We show this code in Ruby because it's easier to see the intention.

```ruby
class RateRepositoryBroker

  def initialize
    @tax_rate_repository_FR = TaxRateRepositoryFR.new
    @tax_rate_repository_US = TaxRateRepositoryUS.new
  end

  def repository_for( country )
    if country == "US"      return @tax_rate_repository_US
    elsif country == "FR"  return @tax_rate_repository_FR
    else  return nil
    end
  end
end
```

```ruby
class TaxCalculator
  def initialize( repository_broker )
    @my_rate_repository_broker = repository_broker
  end
```

```
 def tax_on( country, amount )
  tax_rate_repository = @my_rate_repository_broker.repository_for(
country )
  amount * tax_rate_repository.tax_rate( amount )
 end
end
```

```
class TaxRateRepositoryFR
 def tax_rate( amount )
  0.30
 end
end
```

```
class TaxRateRepositoryUS
 def tax_rate( amount )
  0.15
 end
end
```

```
my_tax_rate_broker = RateRepositoryBroker.new
my_calculator = TaxCalculator.new( my_tax_rate_broker )
puts my_calculator.tax_rate( "FR", 2000 )
puts my_calculator.tax_rate( "US", 2000 )
puts my_calculator.tax_rate( 100 )
```

3.2. Another simple example, the web-hexagon

In the 2010s, Alistair started building a custom content management system in Ruby. To do this, he needed to install and connect to a web service as the driving actor.

He began with the simplest app possible: just returning the input multiplied by a number from a repository. You will recognize this as the tax calculator from the previous example. Since the complexity of the domain was not the concern at that moment, reusing a trivial domain allowed him to create the architecture easily. From there, incorporating Rack was the big step.

The first test uses a mock repository. This is enough to establish the Ports & Adapters architecture. Developing the architecture further with different external technologies, he added Rack for the web on the input side and a flat file for the repository.

After growing the app some more, he simplified it back down to the smallest serviceable example, to show how simple the code is: [https://github.com/totheralistair/SmallerWebHexagon]

Just the app

The app gets configured with the secondary actor through its constructor, setting the repository to use. Because this is coded in Ruby, there are no declarations for the ports.

```ruby
class SmallerWebHexagon

  def initialize rater
    @rater = rater    # the database port needs configuring
  end

  def rate_and_result  value
    rate = @rater.rate(value)
    result = value * rate
    return rate, result
  end
end
```

The first repository: an in-memory repository

To make the tests a bit interesting, we use two tax rates.

```
class InCodeRater

def rate value
  case
    when value <= 100
      1.01
    when value > 100
      1.5
  end
 end

end
```

The first test: test-harness to app to in-memory rater

In this first test, you can see the InCodeRater being passed in with the constructor.

```
class TestRequests < Test::Unit::TestCase
 attr_accessor :app

 def test_it_works_with_in_code_rater
  p __method__
  @app = SmallerWebHexagon.new(InCodeRater.new)
  value_should_produce_rate 100, 1.01
  value_should_produce_rate 200, 1.5
 end
```

At this point the Ports & Adapters architecture has already been completed, there is a primary port for computing taxes, and a secondary one for getting tax rates. Note again that since Ruby does not require interfaces to be declared, the ports themselves are not explicitly visible.

Adding a second type of repository

To test that the architecture functions as intended, we create a file with the tax rates. Alistair likes to use a different number in the file rater, so he can tell which rater is being activated:

```
0   1.0
100 2.0
```

We add a file reader as the adapter:

```ruby
class FileRater

  def initialize fn
    @rates = []
    File.open(fn) do |f|
      f.each_line do |line|
        @rates << line.split.map(&:to_f)
      end
    end
  end
```

```ruby
  def rate value # ugly code but I only need to know it works
    case
      when value >= @rates[0][0] && value < @rates[1][0]
        rate = @rates[0][1]
      when value >= @rates[0][0]
        rate = @rates[1][1]
    end
  end

end
```

Finally, we add a test to ensure all this works.

```ruby
  def test_it_works_with_file_rater
    p __method__
    @app = SmallerWebHexagon.new(FileRater.new('file_rater.txt'))
    value_should_produce_rate 10, 1.00
    value_should_produce_rate 100, 2.0
  end
```

Add a web interface at the front

Finally, we add the interface to Rack for web input:

```ruby
class RackHttpAdapter

  def initialize(hex_app, views_folder)
    @app = hex_app
    @views_folder = views_folder
  end

  def call(env) # hooks into the Rack Request chain
    request = Rack::Request.new(env)
    value =  path_as_number(request)
    rate, result = @app.rate_and_result  value
    out = {
      out_action:  'result_view',
      value: value,
      rate:  rate,
      result: result
    }
    template_path = Pathname.new(
@views_folder).join(out[:out_action]).sub_ext('.erb')
    page = html_from_template_file(template_path , binding)
    response = Rack::Response.new
    response.write(page)
    response.finish
  end
```

To test this, we used the in-memory rater from the first test, then built
the app to run from a browser. This file is "config.ru":

```ruby
# run the Smaller Web Hexagon from a browser

require './src/smaller_web_hexagon'
require './src/rack_http_adapter'
require './src/raters'

hex = SmallerWebHexagon.new(InCodeRater.new)
app = RackHttpAdapter.new(hex,"./src/views/")

run app
```

At this point we can drive the app from the tests or a browser, and get the rates from either the in-memory rater or the file.

The final test suite:

Here is the full set of tests:

```ruby
require_relative '../src/smaller_web_hexagon'
require_relative '../src/rack_http_adapter'
require_relative '../src/raters'
require 'rack/test'
require 'rspec/expectations'
require 'test/unit'

# The first 2 tests check the primary adapter swaps, using direct API access
for the left
# The last test checks the secondary adapter swap, using Rack input.
# The config.ru file runs the real server stuff, for the final usage test.

# note about the tests, I made all the raters give different answers,
# so that I can see if they are hooked up wrong

class TestRequests < Test::Unit::TestCase
  attr_accessor :app

  def test_it_works_with_in_code_rater
    p __method__

    @app = SmallerWebHexagon.new(InCodeRater.new)

    value_should_produce_rate 100, 1.01
    value_should_produce_rate 200, 1.5
  end


  def test_it_works_with_file_rater
    p __method__

    @app = SmallerWebHexagon.new(FileRater.new('file_rater.txt'))

    value_should_produce_rate 10, 1.00
    value_should_produce_rate 100, 2.0
  end
```

```
def test_runs_via_rack_adapter
  p __method__

  views_folder = '../src/views/'
  hex = SmallerWebHexagon.new (InCodeRater.new)
  app = RackHttpAdapter.new(hex, views_folder)

  request = Rack::MockRequest.new(app)
  response = request.request('GET', '/100') # sends the req through the
Rack call(env) chain

  out = {          # expected values
    out_action:  'result_view',
    value:  100,
    rate:  1.01,
    result: (100)*(1.01)
  }
  response.body.should == html_from_template_file(views_folder +
'result_view.erb' , binding)
 end


 def value_should_produce_rate value, exp_rate
   rate, result = @app.rate_and_result value

   rate.should == exp_rate
   result.should == value * exp_rate
 end

end
```

3.3. The BlueZone example

The BlueZone is Juan's full example of how the pattern works.

Note (2025) Juan kept evolving his code, creating two designs in two repositories. A book like this can't keep up with the changes, so in this chapter I'll outline one of his designs, and let you compare the two designs he left. Check:

https://github.com/jmgarridopaz/bluezone

https://github.com/HexArchBook/bluezone_pro

BlueZone allows car drivers to use a web UI to pay for parking at various zones in a city. Different colored lines on the road indicate different parking rates; for example, central downtown is more expensive than a few blocks out. After possibly looking up the rates of different zones, the driver buys a ticket for a zone for a set time, paying by various means.

The parking inspector will check whether parked cars have paid correctly for their zone and time.

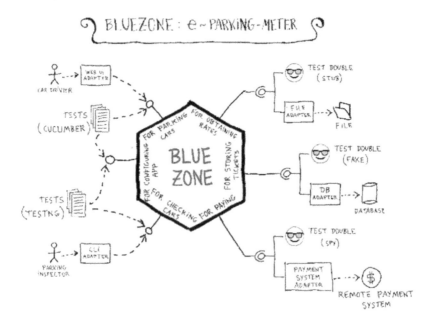

Figure 3.1. The actors in the BlueZone example

The primary (driving) actors are:

* The car driver

* The parking inspector

The secondary (driven) actors are:

* A repository of the different rates for the different zones.

* A repository holding all the tickets.

* A payment service to accept the payments.

Thus there are five ports for two driving actors and three driven actors. We can add one more for configuring work.

The ports are:

* Driving: ForParkingCars

* Driving: ForCheckingCars

* Driven: ForObtainingRates

* Driven: ForStoringTickets

* Driven: ForPaying

* Driving: ForConfiguringApp

The driven actors get set in the app's constructor. Additional configurations options go through the "for configuring" port.

Juan chose different technologies for each of the actors: web for the driver, command line for the inspector, file for the rates, SQL database for the tickets, and payment system gateway for the payments. He also used different test doubles at each port: a stub for the file, a fake for the database, and a spy for the payment gateway. He did this to illustrate different technologies and tests.

Check his repos for details.

Chapter 4:
FAQ – What and How?

4.1. The dinner boat analogy

To help explain the Ports & Adapters architecture, we present an analogy that resembles a setting you might imagine in your day-to-day life.

Consider a dinner boat floating on a river or lake (Figure 4.1). The owners set up a dock to shuttle patrons to and from the restaurant. The dock is officially part of the restaurant. The restaurateurs don't care how their guests arrive at the dock: by car, train, bus, bike, or walking. Once a guest steps onto their shuttle they are considered "in" the restaurant.

The dock is a port into the restaurant. We could name it "for dinner guests", but let's follow our convention and label it "for enjoying dinner." The actor is the "guest", who uses the port "for enjoying dinner."

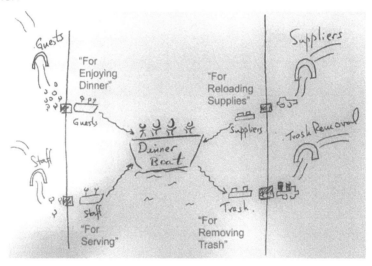

Figure 4.1. The floating restaurant analogy

The restaurant owners don't want their staff to mix with the dinner guests as they come in, so they set up another port, "for serving." The actor is a "staff person," who enters the restaurant through the port labeled "for serving."

"Staff" and "guest" are roles that people occupy at any given moment. If a staff person decides to eat at the dinner boat one night, that person becomes a guest and instead enters at the "for enjoying dinner" port.

The restaurant also wants a port for reloading supplies. To match our Ports & Adapters drawing style, we draw that port on the right-hand bank. Just as how patrons arrive via the "for enjoying dinner" port using different vehicles, suppliers can arrive at the "for reloading supplies" dock via truck, train, helicopter, or whatever.

FInally, we need a port for removing trash from the dinner boat and transporting it to the dump. This port matches a secondary actor who only gets notified of events. Consider it a physical analogy to pagers and emails.

Notice that we have said nothing about how the restaurant is structured internally, nor anything about how anyone gets to the docks. The only design decisions here are that there are four docks, with their specific purposes and any rules attached to the intended traffic at each dock.

See if this analogy helps you solve any issues around your design.

4.2. The hardware chip analogy

Consider a chip in a hardware catalog (see Figure 4.2). When you buy a pre-built chip, you don't get to specify its inputs and outputs. They are already defined by the manufacturer. It is your job to make sure you meet the voltages and timing given in the chip's specs.

Similarly, in Ports & Adapters, the app defines its inputs (the functions the app provides for you to use) and outputs (the functions the app will call). As with the chip, it's your job to meet those contracts.

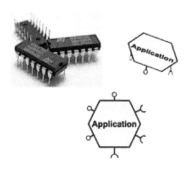

Figure 4.2. The hardware chip analogy

In Figure 4.3, we draw the app as a little hexagon with pins sticking out of it. We draw the input pins with UML's provided-interface lollipop, and the output pins with UML's required-interface socket. As per convention (but not required by any rule), we put the input ports on the left and top and the output ports on the right and bottom. Figure 4.3 shows those pins labeled with the port names "for doing something."

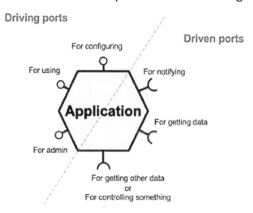

Figure 4.3. Ports are like input and output pins on the chip

The drawing shows our three sorts of common input ports and the three common sorts of output ports. Not every system will have all of these, and some may have more, but this will give you an idea of what you might encounter.

On the input side:

There is obviously a port for the main user of the system. We don't know what type of actor that might be, but generally speaking this port will be "for using" the app. There may, in fact, be several primary actors.

There is often an administrator who adds users, resets passwords, adds things to the database, and so on. That person will have a port "for admining" or some similar name.

Alistair likes to have one port for setting up the secondary actors and doing any other configuration needed by the app. That one is "for configuring." (Note: As described earlier, this port makes the setup clear and lets you swap driven actors live, but it also lets you leave the app in an inconsistent state between the app constructor and the configuring calls.)

On the output side:

There are almost always data repositories to connect with. The ports for those are "for getting data" of various sorts.

There might be pagers and emails to notify. The ports for those will be "for notifying" the devices.

The system might control devices, motors, dispensers and so on. Those ports would be labeled "for controlling" or "for dispensing."

Just as when you wire up a chip in hardware, you have to connect your app to the rest of the world (see Figures 4.4 and 4.5). This is what the configurator does. You might do it in a dependency injection framework like Spring, in the test cases, or in main. The configurator is the "know-it-all" element of the system.

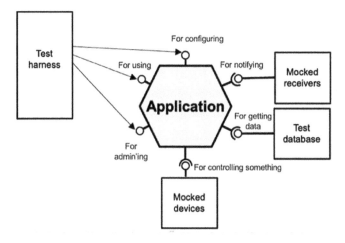

Figure 4.4. Hooking up the connections for testing

Your app's wiring will naturally change when you switch from testing to production. Figure 4.5 shows how the app might be wired up for production; compare this to Figure 4.4, and you'll see that the application never has to be recompiled for these different wirings. The whole point of the Ports & Adapters architecture is that the application is oblivious to the external connections.

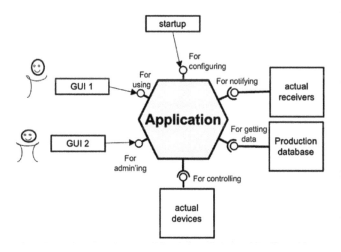

Figure 4.5. Hooking up the connections for production

Speaking of testing, applications have another important similarity to hardware components. The chip manufacturer has to test the component thoroughly before putting it into a catalog. That is an essential part of calling something a "component." For this reason, we come down hard on the testing aspect of the architecture. If you don't have thorough tests around the app, how can you call it a component?

Once you have those tests in place, all sorts of good things follow. One of the benefits of the architecture (above and beyond the advantages in testing) is that the tests keep programmers from leaking business logic into the UI or the databases, or UI or database logic into the business logic.

This test wall is the only way we know to keep the business logic and external interfaces cleanly separated. With the tests, you can detect such faults instantly. Without it, it is nearly impossible.

4.3. What is a port?

The Glossary (Chapter 2.1) defines a port as:

Port: A provided or required interface defined by the app. A port captures the idea of a conversation between an external actor and the app, created for some intention. The name of the port is ideally a description of that intention (e.g., "forPlacingOrders").

The description of port in Pattern Elements (Chapter 2.2) adds this:

The ports define the true boundary of the hexagon.

Every interaction between the app and the outside world happens at a port interface, using the interface language the app itself defines. As such, the ports are the demarcation of what is *inside* the app proper, and what is *outside*.

We organize the interactions between the application and the external actors by the reason they are interacting with the application. In this model, each set of interactions with a given purpose or intention is a *port*.

Here are a few additional notes.

The ports define the totality of the app's external boundary, and therefore belong to the app.

Importantly, a port is not a class. It is the point of interaction defined by the app for external actors. The app declares at a driving port the app's *provided interface* (in UML terms) to its driving actors. The app declares at a driven port the app's *required interface* (in UML terms) to its driven actors.

Some languages, such as Ruby and Python, don't require interfaces to be declared. When programming in these languages, the ports are not visible as separate declarations. It is the programmers' responsibility to see that driving and driven actors use and implement them correctly.

The function names at a port should be technology neutral, named for the business purpose of the interactions.

Please always include a test driver or test double as an external actor at each port, for testing purposes. Without those, there is no real difference between a port (the application's real boundary) and any interface line you draw anywhere on the system diagram.

Finally, Juan advises, from his personal experience:

Make a driven port for an external system, not for a domain concept.

My approach was influenced by Domain Driven Design. When I had a domain concept that depended on an external system, I used to create an interface to abstract the process of building its instances. I gave that interface the driven port role and I gave that process the driven adapter role, no matter how complex the process was, or whether it had to translate the model of the external system into the domain model of my application. This was what DDD calls an "anti-corruption layer."

But Hexagonal Architecture has nothing to do with DDD. Hexagonal Architecture is simply a pattern that says: Put a driven port interface for any "real world thing" (driven actor) that the hexagon needs to talk to.

That was my mistake: I put a driven port for the domain concept, instead of for the external system. I've since learned to make a driven port represent the conversation with an external system, not just the domain concept.

4.4. Where do I put the "app" boundary?

The boundary is determined by the ports. Those define where and in what way anything else can interact with your system. The tests anchor and enforce that definition. The intention of the Ports & Adapters architecture, distinct from Component + Strategy, is that you put that boundary facing external systems.

So what is an "external" system?

An external system is basically one whose interface your team can't change. Any off-the-shelf purchased products, third party libraries, databases, and subsystems defined by other teams, are external systems.

The boundary to the Ports & Adapters system is chosen at those boundaries to protect

* your ability to design your own preferred interfaces to them,

* your ability to test your system without those being present

* your logic from invading or being invaded by them.

In discussions around this question, people often ask whether an in-memory program can be an external system, either driving or driven actor. Of course it can. Once you settle on the boundary to your system and define the ports and their protocols, you can substitute anything you like outside the system to interact with the ports. Tests and test doubles are examples of in-memory actors. It is easy to imagine having other ones.

4.5. How many ports should I have?

As described in *How Does This Relate to Use Cases* (Chapter 5.1), you might start with as many ports as you have primary and secondary actors. You can split actors more finely in use-case modeling, and you can subdivide ports in your architecture, but there is a rapid increase in complexity and decrease in value as you continue splitting. Therefore, we recommend beginning by modelling one port for each primary and secondary actor.

Pay attention to the intention of the conversation at any one port. A driving port supports the fulfillment of one or a set of related goals around a particular intention, and probably a single set of permissions for that conversation. For example, using the Blue Zone parking payment system, the person parking a car has a very different intention, conversation, and permissions than the parking inspector. They will get separate ports.

Inside a company, a sales manager will have different requests and different permissions than a sales clerk. Their specific requests will go through different ports, "for_selling" and "for_managing_sales." Whenever the sales manager wishes to do the activity of a clerk, they would use the port of the clerk for those interactions. At some point they will make a request that the clerk can't make. That will go through the "for_managing_sales" port.

As a designer, you start by looking at the system from a bird's-eye view, identifying and naming the ports from the usage perspective. When you shift to designing the insides of the app, you naturally look at the world from inside the app. You won't care about the nature of that driving actor, or whether it needs an adapter. You care only that a particular service request came in. There is a request for a service, and you design that.

On the driven actor side, the intention of a port is related to:

- the information it needs from a responding secondary actor,

- the information it communicates to an actor that only receives, such as a pager, or

- the controls it activates in a controller.

It is okay to start by calling these ports "for_getting_xyzinfo", "for_notifying_xyzactors", "for_controlling_xyzthing", until you find better ones.

In the end, you are likely to have at least two driving ports and unlikely to have more than seven or eight driven ports, although, of course, systems come in all shapes and sizes. The number of driven ports is determined by the number of external systems you have to connect to.

4.6. How do I structure the inside of my app?

That is totally up to you. "Not my job," as they say. You can make a functional or object-oriented design. You can make a modular monolith or a big ball of mud. You can use "clean architecture", domain-driven design, or anything that suits you. The pattern says exactly nothing on this topic.

Do whatever you prefer. Knock yourself out.

Just one note of warning: You will probably run into difficulty if you try to make hexagons within hexagons, since the Ports & Adapters pattern does not nest. We explore this further in Chapter 5.8, *What About Nested Hexagons?*

4.7. How do I structure my adapters?

As with structuring the inside of the app, the pattern has nothing to say about how you structure your adapters. They are outside.

Have at it.

4.8. Where do I put my files?

The folder structure is not covered by the pattern, nor is it the same in all languages. Some languages (Java), require interface definitions. Some (Python, Ruby) don't. And some, such as Smalltalk, don't even have the concept of files!

That said, we've observed that folder structures that don't match the intentions of the pattern end up causing damage. You can create greater clarity by implementing them in a certain form. Figure 4.6 illustrates.

We offer this section to help you set up the folders so the structure is clear. We describe it for languages needing interfaces to be declared, such as Java and C#. For languages like Python that don't need interface declarations, skip those parts. You will still need the other folders and files.

You will have these directories, modules or projects:

* One for the app business logic and the port definitions,

* Some people prefer to put the ports in another top-level folder, so that adapters need only depend on the interface definitions and not the app,

* One for the driving adapters,

* One for the driven adapters,

* One for the test cases.

If you put the port definitions with the app, you will have 3 subfolders:

* One for the app business logic,

* One to hold the driving port interface definitions,

* One to hold the driven port interface definitions.

If you put the port definitions in a separate top-level folder, be sure to put the driving and driven port definitions in separate folders under that. Practitioners tell me that this is the most important thing in keeping your interface definitions readable. Name the folders using the naming convention "for_doing_something."

Suppose you have two driving ports, one for a user calculating taxes and another for the admin person doing general admin things.

The folders (and also the port and interface) names will be "for_calculating_taxes" and "for_admin_purposes." Actual naming and coding is up to your personal standards, they are not part of the pattern.

For the Test Cases folder, organize as you like.

In the driving adapters and driven adapters folders, make a subfolder for each adapter.

Naming your folders.

As described in the glossary, chapter 2.1, you have several choices for how to name the folders. In this book, we continue to write "Driven/Driving Ports" and "Driven/Driving Adapters." However, some people find those words confusing, so they call the folders "Inbound/Outbout Ports" and "Inbound/Outbound Adapters." A recent proposal was to write: "Provided Interfaces" and 'Required Interfaces." Feel free to use any of these alternatives if you like.

Figure 4.6 shows three ways of setting them up. The top one shows driving/driven port definitions inside the app project. The second has the ports into their own folder. In the third, I show how it looks if you call them Inbound/Outbound. Your choice. These decisions are not mandated by the pattern.

Folder structures that don't match the intentions of the pattern cause confusion and even damage to the project. Create clarity in your project by implementing them in one of these ways.

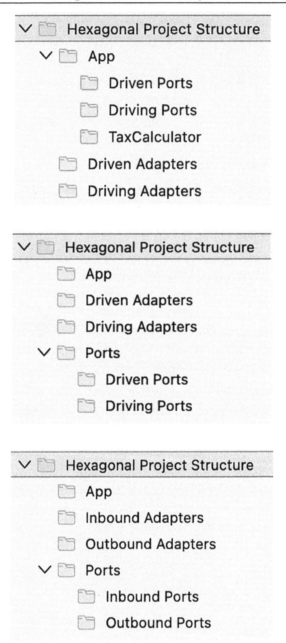

Figure 4.6. Possible folder/project structures.

4.9. What is the development sequence?

The brief description of the development sequence is as follows:

1. Test-to-test: Create the test as the first driver of the app, and connect it to a test double (in memory, mock, stub, fake, etc).

2. Real-to-test: Put the production driver in place, connected to the test double.

3. Test-to-real: Connect tests to the production database, or a test database that uses the same technology as the production database.

4. Real-to-real: Finally, when everything else works, connect the production driver and the production database.

Once you've completed step 1, the architecture is in place. After that, you can do the rest in any order. In particular, steps 2 and 3 might be swapped.

Figure 4-7 shows this sequence.

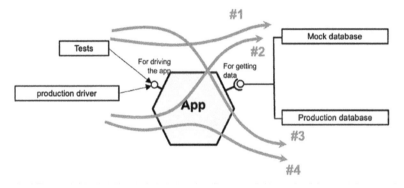

Figure 4-7. The development sequence: Tests and mocks first

The long explanation is not only long, it is different for different languages. The detailed instructions for type-declaring languages like Java are different from non-type-declaring languages like Ruby. As such, we decided it will be easier to follow if they are written out separately.

Here are some notes common to both sequences:

▪ We show the most common configurator, in which you pass the driven actor to the app via the app's constructor. Other configurators are described in detail in section 3 of the article Configurable Receiver (Chapter 6.5).

■ For the folder setup, Alistair's teaching changed the moment he asked people to create the folders before touching any code. Things that had once been confusing to people became straightforward. With the folders in place, it was clear where to put everything. Hence step 0 in both sequences is to set up the folder structure.

■ We recommend using the "Walking Skeleton" pattern (Chapter 6.2) to grow the code. According to this pattern:

  * We first set up the smallest behavior in the app needed to construct and connect the architecture. That is, the first step introduces driving but no driven ports, and has the app only return a constant.

  * The second step introduces one of the driven ports with a test double as the driven actor. At this point the Ports & Adapters architecture has been constructed.

  * Following this, you are free to evolve and grow the app, the ports, the adapters and the external actors in any sequence you like.

Development sequence for type-declared languages

This sequence is for languages such as Java in which you declare types and interfaces.

[0: Preparation] Set up the folder structure

- Create the folders or projects where you will put the app code and the port declarations.

- Create three subfolders there: one for the app business logic, one for "Driving Ports", and one for "Driven Ports."
Alternatively, make the Ports folder separate and at the same level as the App folder or project.

- Outside the app space, in a place that suits your coding conventions, create two folders: "Driving Adapters" and "Driven Adapters."

- Create the folder where you will write your driving tests.

[1: Driving Side] Test the app returning a constant

- Establish the first driving port. Since our purpose here is only to establish the architecture for the driving side, have the app only return a constant: 0, "Hi", or something equally simple. Here's how that goes:

- In "Driving Ports" add a file for your first port/interface declaration. Give the interface a name of the form "ForAccomplishingSomething", for whatever service you intend the app to provide.

- Declare the function signature for a function with no parameters, expecting only a simple value back.

- In the app folder, create the simplest app to service the driving interface. In this first step, it takes no arguments and just returns a constant. It should declare that the app "implements" the driving interface you declared (in whatever language form you need).

- In the test folder, write a test that calls that function and expects that answer. That test code may need to declare that it uses the interface definition, depending on your language and coding conventions.

- Run the test. Hopefully it passes. If not, see what you have to clean up to get the connection to work properly.

Congratulations! At this point, you have already implemented the first driving port in the Ports & Adapters architecture.

Note that this test will end up being thrown away, because all future tests, and the production system, will make use of the driven actors. We have not yet found a way to keep this test running without creating waste code in the final system. With tears in our eyes and chills on our skin, we prepare to comment it out later. It served its purpose.

[2: Driven Side] Test a driven actor returning a constant

Now add a driven port:

- In the "Driven Ports" folder, define just one interface with one function signature for the driven actor. Use the simplest interface possible, ideally with no parameters. Give the interface a name of the sort "ForAccomplishingXYZ", for some service the app needs from its driven actor. This will be the *type* of the arguments and variables holding the driven actor.

- In the "Driven Adapters" folder, add a class that implements the required interface and returns a simple value. You now have your first driven actor. Make sure the code says that it "implements" the required interface.

  Note: This class is a test double. It is actually an actor, not an adapter. To escape ongoing difficulties with terminology here, we use the word 'interactor', to mean "adapter, or actor that doesn't need an adapter." This test double is an example of an actor that doesn't need an adapter.

- Now change the app to use the driven interactor (the test double):

  * Add an instance variable to hold the driven interactor. The type of the instance variable is the driven interface you just defined: "ForAccomplishingXYZ."

  * Add a constructor that accepts a driven interactor as an argument and stores it in the instance variable. The *type* of the argument is the driven interface "ForAccomplishingXYZ", not the driven interactor's class.

* Change the code so that, instead of returning a constant, it asks the driven interactor for the result to use and then returns that.

- Comment out, delete or change the first test case:

  * Create an instance of the new driven interactor (the test double). Declare the type of the driven interactor as the driven interface and not its class.

  * Create the app, passing the driven interactor into the app constructor.

- Test that the app now returns the simple value expected from the test double. We like to use a different value from the first test, to be sure we really made all the correct changes.

Congratulations! You have now implemented the Ports & Adapters architecture! Your system has its first configurator, driving port, driving actor, driven port, driven actor, and the app itself correctly interacts with all of them. From here on, you can evolve the system in any direction you like.

Your next steps will be to put a real UI on the driving side (or connect it to the web or wherever the real driving actor will come from), and to put a real repository or receiver on the driven side, in whichever sequence you prefer.

[3: Driving Side] Add a real driving actor

At this point you are in your own technology. This may be a human interface, a web interface, a microservice, or whatever you choose.

- Add an adapter, if that is needed, in the "Driving Adapters" folder. You may need an adapter for a web interface, and you might not need an adapter to use your app as a microservice. You will have your own preferred place to put a UI to a human. At this point, it's up to you how you work.

- You may need to declare that your adapter, or driving actor, "uses" the driving port definition.

At the end of step 3, you have two drivers for the system which is still only connected to your test double.

[4: Driven Side] Add a real repository or receiver

- Choose a technology for your driven actor. This may be a file with data, a database interface, access to the web, or whatever you deem appropriate.

- Add an adapter to the "Driven Adapters" folder that declares and implements the same driven interface. Add the repository or receiver wherever appropriate for you.

At this point, you have multiple driving and driven actors. The architecture is in play.

- Add more driving and driven ports and actors on each side as you need.

Development sequence for non-type-declared languages

The following is for languages such as Ruby in which you don't have to declare types and interfaces. As before, we chose the most common configurator, in which you pass in the driven actor via the app's constructor, we set up the folder structure first, and we use the Walking Skeleton pattern.

[0: Preparation] Set up the folder structure

- Create the folder where you will put the app code.

- Outside the app space, in a place that suits your coding conventions, create two folders: "driving_adapters" and "driven_adapters."

- Create the folder where you will write your driving tests.

[1: Driving Side] Just test the app returning a constant

- Establish the first driving actor. Since our purpose here is only to establish the architecture for the driving side, have the app only return a constant: 0, "Hi", or something equally simple. Here's how that goes:

- In the app folder, create the simplest app to service the driving interface. In this first step, it takes no arguments and just returns a constant.

- In the test folder, write a test that calls that function and expects that constant.

- Run the test. Hopefully it passes. If not, see what you have to clean up to get the connection to work properly.

Congratulations! At this point, you have already implemented the first driving port in the Ports & Adapters architecture.

Note that this test will end up being thrown away, because all future tests, and the production system, will make use of the driven actors. We have not yet found a way to keep this test running without creating waste code in the final system. With tears in our eyes and chills on our skin, we prepare to comment it out later. It served its purpose.

[2: Driven Side] Test a driven actor returning a constant

Now add a driven actor:

- In the "driven_adapters" folder, add a class that implements the required interface and returns a simple value. You now have your first driven actor.

  Note: This class is a test double. It is actually an actor, not an adapter. To escape ongoing difficulties with terminology here, we use the word 'interactor', to mean "adapter, or actor that doesn't need an adapter." This test double is an example of an actor that doesn't need an adapter

- Next, change the app to use the driven interactor:

  * Add an instance variable to hold the driven interactor.

  * Add a constructor that accepts a driven interactor as an argument and stores it in the instance variable.

  * Change the code so that, instead of returning a constant, it asks the driven interactor for the result to use and then returns that.

- Comment out, delete or change the first test case:

  * Create an instance of the new driven interactor (the test double).

  * Create the app, passing the driven interactor into the app constructor.

- Test that the app now returns the simple value expected from the driven actor. We like to use a different value from the first test, to be sure we really made all the correct changes.

Congratulations! You have now implemented the Ports & Adapters architecture. Your baby system has its first configurator, driving port, driving actor, driven port, driven actor, and the app itself correctly interacts with all of them. From here on, you can evolve the system in any direction you like.

Your next steps will be to put a real UI on the driving side (or connect it to the web or wherever the real driving actor will come from), and to put a real repository or receiver on the driven side, in whichever sequence you prefer.

Shortening the descriptions, they look like this:

[3: Driving Side] Add a real driving actor

At this point you are in your own technology. This may be a human interface, a web interface, a microservice, or whatever you choose.

- Add an adapter, if that is needed, in the "driving_adapters" folder. You may need an adapter for a web interface, and you might not need an adapter to use your app as a microservice. You will have your own preferred place to put a UI to a human. At this point it's up to you how you work.

At the end of step 3, you have two drivers for the system. Both should be connected to your test double.

[4: Driven Side] Add a real repository or receiver

- Choose a technology for your driven actor. This may be a file with data, a database interface, access to the web, or whatever you deem appropriate.

- Add an adapter to the "driven_adapters" folder. Add the repository or receiver wherever appropriate for you.

At this point, you have two driving and two driven actors. The architecture is in play. Add more driving and driven ports and actors on each side as you need.

Chapter 5:
FAQ – Related Concepts

5.1. How does this relate to use cases?

There is a surprising relation between Ports & Adapters and use cases. Let's start with some vocabulary, which we will use to connect the two:

A *system under design* (SuD) can be any system, all hardware, all software, an organization, or any combination of those.

An *actor* is anything with behavior. Again, this can be any combination of hardware, software, humans, or organization.

A *primary actor* is any actor that drives the SuD. The primary actor has a goal to achieve and calls upon a service promise of the SuD in order to achieve that goal. The key element here is that the SuD, sitting in a quiet state, is kicked into action via a request from the primary actor.

A *secondary actor* is any actor being driven by the SuD. The key point here is that the SuD is not sitting in a quiescent state, but is actively achieving its own goals as a response to a request from a primary actor, and needs the services of this other actor. The SuD calls upon a service promise of the secondary actor.

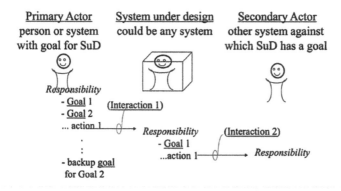

Figure 5.1. Primary and secondary actors and their goals

The only real difference between primary and secondary actors is who initiates their conversation. That conversation may run over multiple interactions.

In use-case modeling a company or system, we start by creating one primary actor for every job role that will be using the system. Clerks, for example, have different needs and permissions than external customers, and managers have different needs and permissions than clerks. Technicians, support people, and so on, will each have different goals and permissions.

An automated system may stand in for a human to drive the system. In these cases, we use a role-name to cover them both.

The trigger to the system may be time-based, such as midnight, every morning at 7:00 a.m., or the end of the month. In these cases, the primary actor is considered to be the person who would request that service if they didn't have the help of the automated timer.

It is common to have anywhere from three to eight or so primary actors, although the number varies by system and situation. Those might include the organization-external users, the organization-internal users, the tech support staff, certain automated systems, and so on.

The number of secondary actors varies from one or two for simple systems to perhaps a dozen for larger systems.

Exactly as for the Ports & Adapters architecture, every actor is there for a purpose, either requesting or providing services as part of fulfilling their goals. That purpose may involve multiple calls or interactions.

We hope you see how closely all this matches the structure of the Ports & Adapters architecture. The "system under design" in use cases is what we are calling the app. Primary actors in use-case language are driving actors in Ports & Adapters language. Secondary actors are driven actors.

The concept of ports doesn't exist in use-case modeling. Even so, it is natural (at least to start with) to give each external actor their own port, named for the general intention of their particular conversation. You may decide to split ports more finely, but be careful; just as primary actors in use cases can be split into so many fragments that they are no longer useful, so the same applies to ports.

Adapters are not mentioned in use cases, because use cases only discuss the activities at each port, saying nothing about external actors.

To learn more about use cases, see
Writing Effective Use Cases (Alistair Cockburn, 2000, Addison-Wesley) or *Unifying User Stories, Use Cases and Story Maps* (Alistair Cockburn, 2024, Humans and Technology Press).

5.2. How does this relate to *Walking Skeleton*?

Walking Skeleton is a project management pattern that works well with *Ports & Adapters*:

> A Walking Skeleton is a tiny implementation of the system that performs a small end-to-end function. It need not use the final architecture, but it should link together the main architectural components. The architecture and the functionality can then evolve in parallel.
> (https://web.archive.org/web/20140329201356/http://alistair.cockb urn.us/Walking+skeleton)

Where Ports & Adapters defines the architecture that will be used, Walking Skeleton advises on the process of building it. It advises against building the whole application at once, even using only the test harnesses (Step 1 in the development sequence). Instead, it advises to first create the initial nearly-empty transaction in the tests, then to connect the real technologies for that nearly-empty transaction.

This choice is primarily a risk-management decision. Difficulties and mixups are common when connecting the final technologies. Getting those technologies connected early—for me, immediately after setting up the Ports & Adapters architecture for a nearly-empty transaction— allows you to check for those complications, and immediately sets up your test and delivery pipelines.

You don't have to use Walking Skeleton. In fact, we only mentioned it in the detailed explanation for the development sequence:

[1: Driving Side] Just test the app returning a constant

[2: Driven Side] Test a driven actor returning a constant

[3: Driving Side] Add a real driving actor

[4: Driven Side] Add a real repository or receiver

For me (Alistair), implementing Walking Skeleton is second nature. I apply it automatically and don't notice that others find this surprising.

Juan, however, was totally unaware of this strategy, and wrote all the BlueZone code with just the tests, and started changing the technologies after that. He only noticed the Walking Skeleton pattern after he was done, just a month before this book was to go to press! All this time, he had been confused by my adding in the real technologies so early in my talks.

Here are his notes to me as he came to understand the differences and the interplays between the two:

> my takeaway is the following:

> the point is how much business logic do you implement in the step 2... it doesn't say anywhere that first you just implement a tiny functionality for the WS.... on the other hand, you can even implement the whole business logic in step 2 before connecting real things outside... it isn't said anywhere.

> reading the dev seq, i thought that in step 1, with all the tests around, the app (business logic) was completely implemented, and then real things were added alternatively at both sides.

> but i was wrong in this. you can do little tiny impl in step 1, add real things in steps 2,3,4.... and then back to step 1 again.

> i wonder if more people have this misconception also.

Yes, I'm sure they do. Thanks again, Juan, for clearing up some misconceptions.

5.3. Is the pattern symmetric or asymmetric?

The pattern is symmetric, the implementation is asymmetric.

The pattern says, "Put an API around everywhere and separate the inside from the outside, regardless of whether the interfaces are for input or output, primary or secondary."

This is the symmetric part.

Patterns such as Model-View-Controller and its siblings regulate only the driving side. It is possible to implement them correctly and still have a tight coupling between the business logic and the database or other secondary actors.

Ports & Adapters differs in that it says the app can have no knowledge of what its external connections are made of, no matter whether they are driving or driven. No compile-time dependencies point from the app to the external actors, anywhere.

When it comes time to implement the pattern, the left-right asymmetry arises. The driving actors have to know of the app to call it, while the app has to know of the secondary actors to call them. Although the app may never know its driving actors, the configurator has to hand the app the secondary actors to use at the driven ports. This causes an asymmetry in the code, making for *provided* interfaces at the driving ports and *required* interfaces at the driven ports.

Thus, the pattern itself is symmetric, and the implementation is asymmetric.

5.4. Is the test suite a driving actor or an adapter?

The difficulty in providing a simple answer to this question is that a single standalone test case is different from a test suite, and different again from a test framework running test data. Juan and I debated this for weeks before arriving at a view that suited us both.

In the first stage of development, you might write a simple test case that instantiates the app, configures it with a secondary actor, calls a function, checks the result, then finally uses a testing framework to announce whether the test passes or fails. The test case is hardcoded to the driving port, and hence needs no adapter.

Over time, you create a repository of test data containing the inputs and expected outputs. One loosely calls those the "test cases", although they might just be data tables. Since the data tables themselves have no behavior, the test cases are neither the driver nor the adapter.

You probably use a framework to read the data specs, drive the app, check the outputs and publish the results. That framework knows nothing about the driving port's provided interface, so it is not an adapter. Rather, through its use of how you tell it to use the test specs, it manages to meet the driving port's provided interface. No separate adapter is needed between the testing framework and the app. Once again, there is no "adapter."

Is there ever an adapter? And if so, do we need to split the discussion of the various testing situations to separate those in which there is an adapter from those in which there isn't?

We spent weeks on this discussion, splitting hairs about test cases, test data, test harness, and so on. We finally concluded that the energy is not well spent, and that it suffices to use the term "test cases" to mean any of the above. Is one term better than another? We honestly don't really care which you use, because it won't make any difference: you will still define ports, provided interfaces, and required interfaces, which will be used by actors and adapters in some combination. The app does not know or care whether an adapter was used.

We therefore decided to draw "the tests" as a driving actor with no reference to adapters. The phrase "test double" means the same when referring to driven actors, that is, any constellation of elements that meets the driven port requirements.

5.5. Layered, onion, clean, hexagonal: what is the difference?

The Ports & Adapters architecture differs from layered, onion and clean architectures in two ways:

- Ports & Adapters has only two layers: the inside (the app), and the outside (everything else).
- Ports & Adapters requires that you organize the external actors so they connect to specific ports.

But let's look at conventional layered architectures first. In a layered architecture, you separate code by concerns and arrange them from "higher" and "lower," such that higher-level items call or have a dependency upon lower-level ones. More abstract concerns like policy objects are placed higher in the architecture, while hardware and drivers sit on the bottom. The policy items have dependency on the drivers and hardware.

Ports & Adapters, onion, and clean architectures all put the application and domain *below* the UI and infrastructure, as Figure 5.2 illustrates. This makes them appear upside down compared to traditional layered architecture pictures.

The inside of the app with the policy items is on the bottom. Everything else is *above* it, pointing downward. That is because the app can't have a compile-time dependency on anything else.

Inside the upper layer, the "outside", you may have any number of layers of your own choosing. Those decisions are outside the Ports & Adapters architecture and are your personal choices.

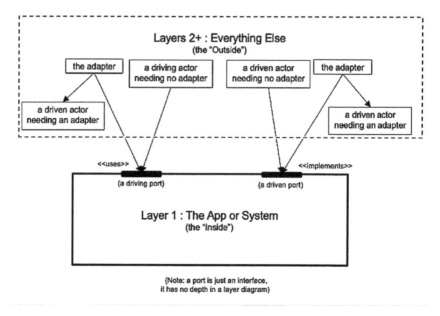

Figure 5.2. Ports & Adapters only specifies two layers: inside and outside.

Figures 5.3 and 5.4 show why the Ports & Adapters architecture looks strange when you are used to a layered architecture.

Figure 5.3 shows an invoicing system with a GUI and a database. On the left is the usual 3-layer architecture with dependencies pointing downward. The execution calls also go down.

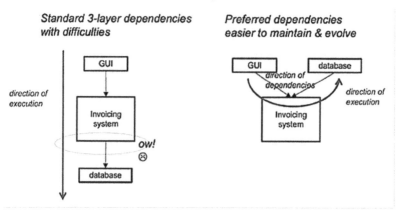

Figure 5.3. Order of dependencies and execution in 3-layer versus Ports & Adapters architectures.

On the right is the Ports & Adapters architecture. As with Figure 5.2, the invoicing system is on the bottom, with both the GUI and the database (or its adapter) having a compile-time dependency on the invoicing system.

What is surprising is that the execution sequence goes in the opposite direction of the dependencies on the driven side. The invoicing system still sends calls to the database, but the database (or its adapter) has the compile-time dependency on the invoicing system. This is different to a layered architecture.

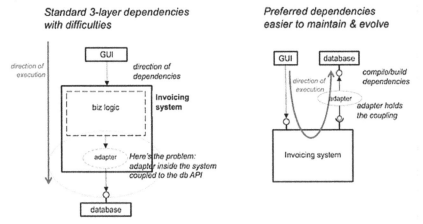

Figure 5.4. Moving the adapter outside and making it dependent on both the system and the database.

Figure 5.4 shows the adapters. The database being purchased has its own published interface, which doesn't match the domain interface of the system under design. An adapter is needed. Usually, that adapter is considered part of the system being designed. Both the compile-time dependencies and the execution flow go from the business logic to the adapter, to the database. This is shown on the left side.

The right side shows the dependencies and execution in the Ports & Adapters architecture. Note that the adapter is outside the system.

- The system publishes its driven port specification (the hook going upward in the drawing);
- the adapter has a compile-time dependency on and implements that interface (the ball fits into the hook);
- the adapter also has a compile-time dependency on and uses the database defined interface.

Note that neither the invoicing system nor the database depend on each other – they are independent. The adapter depends on both of them. The execution flows from the invoicing system to the adapter to the database (and back again).

James Grenning's Embedded IoT

In a parallel evolution, James Grenning (another author of the Agile Manifesto) developed the exact same architecture as Ports & Adapters for systems involving hardware. We found our two designs identical, just using different words. Notable to me was his referring to the driven adapters as the "Service Abstraction Layer," which seems just right.

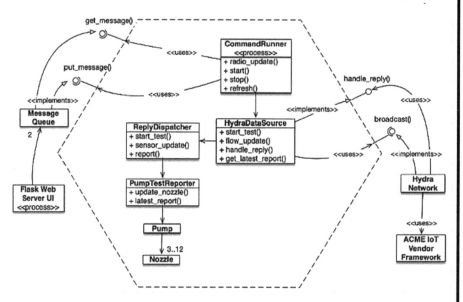

Figure 5.5. Grenning's IoT system.

His sample diagram confused me for a bit, because the 'get' to the message queue is a driven port! That worried me, until he told me that the message queue is polled: the app sends a 'get' request every second. So the ports are correct.

See his full writeup, with code in Python, in Chapter 8 of the forthcoming *Clean Code: A Handbook of Agile Software Craftsmanship, 2nd Ed* (2025).

Onion and Clean

Onion and Clean have the same dependency structure as Ports & Adapters. The two differences are that they don't require the specification of ports, and they do call for additional layers that Ports & Adapters doesn't. Figures 5.5 and 5.6 show these layers.

Once you have implemented Ports & Adapters, you are welcome to add the layers of clean and onion – or not. Those decisions are outside Ports & Adapters. Your choice.

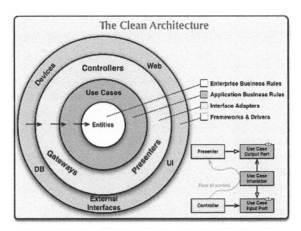

Figure 5.6. Clean architecture
https://blog.cleancoder.com/uncle-bob/2012/08/13/the-clean-architecture.html

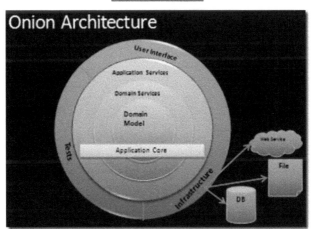

Figure 5.7. Onion architecture
https://jeffreypalermo.com/2008/07/the-onion-architecture-part-1/

If you're feeling bombarded by drawings right now, don't worry. Recall the wisdom of David Adamo Jr: The code is simpler than the drawings.

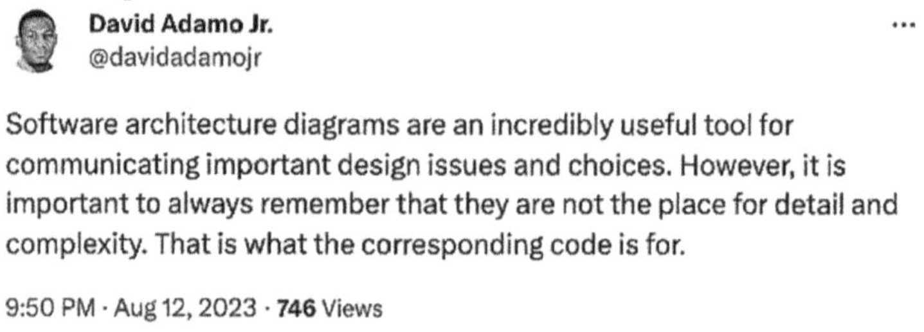

 David Adamo Jr.
@davidadamojr   ...

Software architecture diagrams are an incredibly useful tool for communicating important design issues and choices. However, it is important to always remember that they are not the place for detail and complexity. That is what the corresponding code is for.

9:50 PM · Aug 12, 2023 · **746** Views

Figure 5.8. Architecture drawings are not code:
https://twitter.com/davidadamojr/status/1690541235918753792

Remember, in Ports & Adapters you are free to organize the inside of the app in any way you like, and the things outside the app in any way you like.

Just put ports in place. Oh, and write those tests.

Moving from Layered to Ports & Adapters.

Oliver Zihler published a wonderful article on Substack
[https://codeartify.substack.com/p/from-layered-to-hexagonal-architecture] "From
Layered to Hexagonal Architecture in 2 steps", which describes it
clearly. Here are his figures. Read the article for his explanation if it is
not evident how to interpret them.

Step 0: Your starting point:

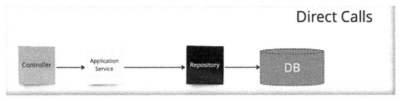

Step 1: Invert dependencies:

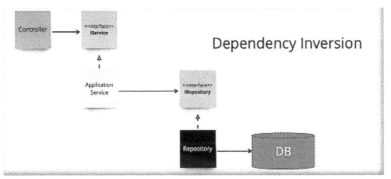

Step 2: Make sure the ports are defined inside the app. Done.

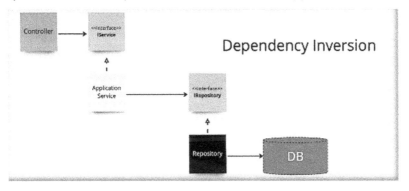

Figure 5.9. From Layered to Hexagonal Architecture in 2 steps
(Figures copyright Oliver Zihler)

5.6. How does this relate to DDD?

Domain-Driven Design (DDD) and Ports & Adapters are different concepts. They were created independently and evolved separately. While the two architectural patterns are not actually related nor explicitly tied to one another, they are compatible. You can use Ports & Adapters without doing DDD, and you can do DDD without using Ports & Adapters. As it turns out, they work really well together.

Consider Ports & Adapters as an architectural *precursor* to DDD, as it will simplify your DDD work. As Eric Evans wrote in Getting Started with DDD When Surrounded by Legacy Systems:

> "...effectively applying the tactical techniques of DDD requires a clean, bounded context. This can be a daunting requirement when your work is dominated by legacy systems. These systems are often tangled..."
> — Evans, [https://www.domainlanguage.com/wp-content/uploads/2016/04/GettingStartedWithDDDWhenSurroundedByLegacySystemsV1.pdf]

Ports & Adapters simplifies that entanglement. It puts all external technologies outside the app, so that the inside only contains domain concepts. From there, you can do your domain-driven design without distraction.

Recall that Ports & Adapters does not constrain your internal design of the app. You are welcome to use domain-driven design or not, as you choose. For this reason, as with clean and onion architectures, we do not discuss the internal structuring of a domain-driven design.

Watch Eric Evans's 2019 lecture on bounded contexts here: [https://www.youtube.com/watch?v=xyuKx5HsGK8]

Are DDD's "Bounded Contexts" hexagons?

Remember first of all that hexagons, *per se*, don't exist. Merely drawing a hexagon on a diagram does not actually mean anything. Ports with provided and required interfaces are the things that actually exist.

This question therefore becomes two questions:

Can a bounded context have ports?
(Yes, it can.)

Are all bounded contexts implementations of the Ports & Adapters architecture?
(No, they aren't.)

Let's look closer:

A "bounded context" in DDD terminology is:

> "...a logical boundary of a domain where particular terms and rules apply consistently. Inside this boundary, all terms, definitions, and concepts form the Ubiquitous Language. In particular, the main benefit of ubiquitous language is grouping together project members from different areas around a specific business domain. Additionally, multiple [bounded] contexts may work with the same thing. However, it may have different meanings inside each of these [bounded] contexts."
> -- [https://www.baeldung.com/java-modules-ddd-bounded-contexts]

Notice that the definition of a bounded context does not say anything about ports or interfaces. Only that it is a logical boundary, a grouping of elements where the meaning of a term is agreed upon.

What makes a "port"? Ports, which belong to the app, define the app's external boundary, in turn defining the interfaces into or out of the app.

As described in *"Component + Strategy generalizes Ports & Adapters"* (Chapter 6.4), the important thing is that the selected area is treated as a component, with ports and test cases at the boundary. The tests achieve multiple things:

They demonstrate that you are serious about the boundary. It is not just any line drawn around any set of classes, but concretely identifies an app or system you wish to be considered as a whole. Not having tests means the people on the project don't consider this to be the boundary to protect.

The tests force the issue of having clean interfaces on both the driving and driven sides, so that you can change external technology easily. If your bounded context has no tests, you have a nice drawing but not much more. You are not protecting anything of interest.

The next question becomes: Does the bounded context define and own both the provided and required interfaces? If not, then the bounded context is dependent on external entities, violating the Component + Strategy pattern (and by implication, violated Ports & Adapters). Your design might have a bounded context connected to an anti-corruption layer (ACL), but if the bounded context knows of the ACL, it is dependent on it.

The final question is: Do you have test drivers or doubles on all the ports? If so, then you have protected your bounded context, and you have implemented the Component + Strategy pattern.

You may or may not have implemented Ports & Adapters. The Ports & Adapters architecture is a particular case of Component + Strategy in which the boundary of the system being protected is where technology elements connect to the app, or a team's decision-making authority ends (see Section 4.5, *FAQ: Where do I put the app boundary?*) You might use several bounded contexts inside this area.

In terms of development sequence, Ports & Adapters simplifies the entanglement mentioned above. It puts all external technologies outside the app, so that the inside only contains domain concepts. From there, you can do your domain-driven design without distraction, placing layers and bounded contexts inside the boundary as suits your needs. Each bounded context does not even have to be a Component + Strategy implementation, but might simply be a logical grouping of domain concepts. As described in Section 4.7, "How do I structure the inside of my app?", you can do whatever you like.

Are Anti-Corruption Layers the adapters of Ports & Adapters?

The answer is "maybe." Explaining this gets complicated, so we provide a short answer here and an in-depth explanation in the next section.

Anti-corruption layers (ACLs) attach to bounded contexts in much the same way as adapters do in the Ports & Adapters architecture. So, are they really the same?

Recall that in the Ports & Adapters architecture, adapters are outside the app boundary and the tests of the app do not include the adapters.

An anti-corruption layer (ACL) is a translator between two modeling languages. If the two bounded contexts are designed to fit the

"Component + Strategy" pattern, with defined interfaces and tests, then it makes sense to consider the ACL an adapter.

If a bounded context doesn't have ports around it, with tests for those ports, then that bounded context doesn't capture a system boundary as is needed for Ports & Adapters. In this case, the anti-corruption layer is still part of the "system," using the terms in this book.

This brings us back to the question about where to put the edge of the hexagon. As mentioned in Section 6.5, The Article "Configurable Receiver", there are times when the project or product is large and developed by many teams. Each team has its defined area where it can make decisions about how other teams can interact with their subsystem. In this case, each team may implement Component + Strategy for their subsystem, with ports and tests. They will treat the ACL as outside their system, i.e. as an external adapter.

5.7. DDD's anti-corruption layers

The anti-corruption layer (ACL) concept from domain-driven design is broader than the adapter from Ports & Adapters. Some parts of an ACL may sit inside a Ports & Adapters system, and some may sit outside.

As Eric Evans wrote in Getting Started with DDD When Surrounded by Legacy Systems:

> "data is coming from one or more legacy systems. We query the legacy database and rearrange the data into the new concepts in the ACL."

> "working out the translation is an important part of the analysis when using an anticorruption layer. The implementation of that translator can take many forms. As much as practical, it should be kept loosely coupled to the rest of the ACL."
>
> -- [https://www.domainlanguage.com/wp-content/uploads/2016/04/GettingStartedWithDDDWhenSurroundedByLegacySystemsV1.pdf]

Figure 5.10 shows an example borrowed from page 7 of his article.

But where is the system boundary? That depends on how you define your ports and where you put your tests.

Tests make a line drawn around a subsystem real. Without the tests, you can draw a line anywhere without any implications. The tests define the real boundary.

The Component+Strategy pattern lets you draw the line anywhere you like, as long as you define ports and have those tests. You can make each bounded context its own component, define the ports, write the tests, put the ACLs outside all of them, translating between them. However, we've found that most teams don't have the energy for all that extra work. As a consequence, that does make Ports & Adapters.

Although you *can* put ports and boundaries around every bounded context, the Ports & Adapters pattern is really aimed at protecting your team from external technology shifts. Thus, the pattern suggests placing the system boundary just in front of each external technology, keeping the adapters simpler.

The advantage of such a boundary is that the team is much more likely to maintain the tests at that boundary than at others.

If you do this, you might find that your anti-corruption layer sits both partially outside and partially inside the system, as shown below:

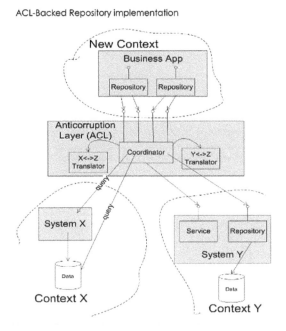

Figure 5.10. Example of an ACL with several responsibilities (Evans, E, 2013)

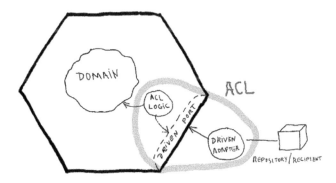

Figure 5.11: Anti-corruption layer blending over the hexagon boundary

Does that look a bit strange to you? It does to us, too. This is why we focus so much on the tests. You can draw a line around any part of your code and call it anything you like, but only when you have to maintain the tests do boundaries become real.

5.8. What about nested hexagons?

As described in the article *Component + Strategy generalizes Ports & Adapters* (see Chapter 6.4), you can nest the Component + Strategy pattern, assuming you really write the tests. You can have components within components if you like, assuming you meet the criteria.

The Ports & Adapters pattern is aimed at protecting your team from external technology shifts. The pattern suggests declaring the system boundary just in front of each external technology. For more information, see Chapter 4.5, *Where do I put the 'app' boundary?*

As such, we say that the Hexagonal or Ports & Adapters architecture does not nest.

5.9. Is CQRS an example of Ports & Adapters?

Command-Query Responsibility Separation (CQRS) is an interesting architecture created by Greg Young. See [https://cqrs.files.wordpress.com/2010/11/cqrs_documents.pdf]

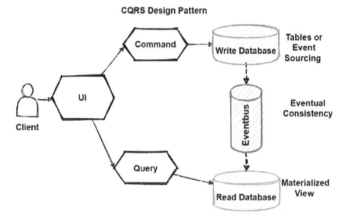

Figure 5.12. The CQRS architecture, courtesy of Mehmet Ozkaya [https://medium.com/design-microservices-architecture-with-patterns/cqrs-design-pattern-in-microservices-architectures-5d41e359768c}

In a lightning talk at Mountain West Rubyconf 2010, Alistair presented the CQRS architecture and asked if it was an example of Hexagonal Architecture. Pat Maddox, at the conference, sat with Alistair later. Together they worked through the evolution of a CQRS architecture and related design patterns. The conclusion was that CQRS might use Ports & Adapters, but it was not, in itself, an example of Ports & Adapters. See [https://www.youtube.com/watch?v=9kQ2veoeWZM].

Both Command and Query sections of CQRS are bounded subsystems. If they are decoupled from the driving and driven technologies, then they form examples of Ports & Adapters. We write "if", because there is nothing in the CQRS architecture to prevent you from coupling those elements directly to the technologies and having the same difficulties as any other system design with such direct coupling.

These are great examples of how to use the Ports & Adapters architecture in a larger system. However, a total CQRS system is composed not only of those business logic parts, but also of the external technology parts, specifically the repositories and the UI. The total system itself is not an example of Ports & Adapters.

Chapter 6:
The Original Articles

6.1. The longer history

One of the last contributions Juan made to this book was to go back and clean up the timeline. I remain grateful to him for his attention to detail and correctness.

To be clear about one point about this history: I am not a systems programmer, I have always been an application programmer. But I grew up with Smalltalk's Model-View-Controller on the driving side, being able to swap drivers easily. I simply assumed and expected that I should be able to do the same on the driven side. I kept asking for this capability of the system architects and being told it wasn't possible. It was out of defense that I started asking myself, How should things be done so that it would be possible? I called it *shunt* at first, and then *loopback* (mocks weren't invented then), came up with the idea of how to do it, and finally in 2004-2005 was in a situation to write some code that did it.

In other words, I created this architecture so that I, as an application programmer, could have those safety /swapping features I needed to develop the application.

1988: Smalltalk and C

Alistair unknowingly implemented Model-View-Controller in his Smalltalk prototype, but his C programmer didn't. When the need arose to change the source of inputs, that program had to be torn apart and rewritten.

At IBM Research in Switzerland, I had just learned Smalltalk for a new project, with a pre-doctoral student on my team who would implement what my Smalltalk prototype did into a properly fast diagram editor in C.

The Smalltalk tutorial had me code up a "talking parrot", to get us used to state machines. As it turned out, not to my knowledge at the time, that example used the Model-View-Controller architecture. When I made my first real program, I simply copied the talking parrot example and changed it to fit my needs. (There is a separate lesson in here about how to learn a new language, but we can leave that out for now.) As a result, I had the MVC structure in my code without knowing it.

My pre-doc, of course, did not know this pattern (nor did I, to be honest). He programmed in C.

The program he wrote was a graphical editor for editing message-flow sequences between computers on a network.

We had imagined there would be between 10 and 30 messages on a diagram, since they would be drawn by hand. However, our very first customer got all excited about this editor - they could see how to use it to visualize really large network logs that contained an error somewhere. Their very first use of it had about 120 different server stations horizontally and thousands of messages.

Needless to say, that broke his program. It was hard-coded to talk to a graphical user interface with a person and a mouse, not the network or a data file. Looking at my Smalltalk program, I said, "Just make the input come from the network instead of the keyboard." (This is a standard MVC move.) He looked at me strangely, and said he couldn't do that, he would have to start over.

I was confused. Why couldn't he just change the input source?

Years later, I finally understood that the MVC architecture had forced me to create a program interface for all inputs. With this, I could change the input sources any way I wanted. Test cases, GUI, network input, all were equally possible.

This experience taught me to value surrounding my app with interfaces.

1994: Smalltalk and relational databases

On a fixed-price, fixed-time project involving an object-relational mapper, the infrastructure designers found they had to change their design to the SQL database to improve performance. Not being able to allow the application programmers to substitute an in-memory test database, they shut down the project for several weeks while they frantically rewrote their mapper.

Alistair draws for the first time the hexagon shape, in the slides of his class about object-oriented programming.

The critical event that pushed me into finding the Ports & Adapters architecture was a project in 1994-95, which had a Smalltalk front end connected to a relational database.

The first implementation of the object-to-relational mapper was very coding intensive and slow. The infrastructure team decided they had to completely redo the mapper. They needed several weeks to revise the architecture.

I asked the infrastructure team to just give us the API and we would fake the back end, using loopbacks to have little tests while we coded.

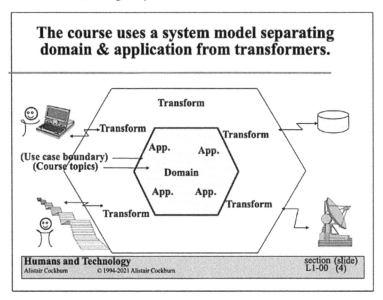

Figure 6.1. The earliest hexagonal picture, from 1994

They said the same thing my C programmer had said six years earlier, "Can't do that, no idea what you're talking about." They shut down function development for weeks while they reprogrammed the database interface.

Had they put a "required interface" at that back-end boundary, we could have all kept going. I didn't have the words at the time to describe either what I wanted or how to do it, I just knew it was possible and the proper way to design.

During that project, I taught the team a week-long class, "Design in Object Technology" (now a *book*). It already had the hexagonal shape (see Figure 6.1), and the basic concept was in place, although I didn't really know what the facets meant. I knew they had to be there, they had to be APIs, but I couldn't say more.

2000: Mho's weather system

Alistair visited a friend who was having trouble with all the variants and versions of his application, with different input sources and notification methods. Those problems were solved with this architecture.

While I was visiting my friend Mho Salim sometime around 2000, he described what he was working on and the current problem he was wrestling with.

His weather-alert system took in weather feeds from the National Oceanic and Atmospheric Administration (NOAA) and other sources. and using database of subscribers with their phone numbers, his system would call them up when there was a weather alert relevant to them, and leave a message on their voice-answering system. (This was the late 1990s, remember.)

His problem was that the internet was starting, and he was creating a different, custom system for every technology variation. Inputs were coming from direct feeds, RSS feeds, and the internet. Outgoing messages were going as voice to analog phone-answering machines, as text to pagers, and starting to go to RSS feeds, with possibility for internet. On top of that, he was starting work on a sister app that would interface directly with this system.

Looking at all the combinations and permutations of those technologies, he was despairing of the upcoming maintenance and evolution work on the program.

Steeped in APIs as I was, I couldn't see the problem. I drew something like this on his whiteboard (see Figure 6.2).

I still didn't have words to describe all the elements. I only knew, as a colleague once said, "Give me API or give me death!" (Oblique reference to the American revolutionary war, for those not familiar with the original saying.)

Mho just looked at me strangely. This was evidently a new way of thinking for him.

After that conversation, I got more serious about trying to work out just what this thing was that I assumed people would do.

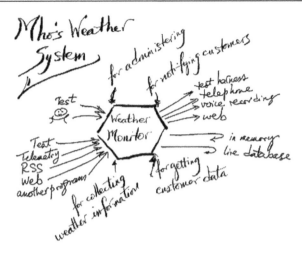

Figure 6.2. Mho's weather system in the hexagon

2003: First publication on Ward Cunningham's wikiwiki web

Alistair publishes an article titled "Hexagonal Architecture" in Ward Cunningham's "Wiki Wiki Web."
[https://web.archive.org/web/20030320101333/http://www.c2.com/cgi/wiki?HexagonalArchitecture]

2005: Ports & Adapters

September 4, 2005: Alistair writes the pattern formally according to the GoF (Gang of Four) format and gives it the correct name: "Ports & Adapters." He publishes the article on his web site on September 5, 2005, and sends out an RSS with the announcement of what and why.

Alistair adds the article to Ward's wiki:
[http://wiki.c2.com/?PortsAndAdaptersArchitecture]

In 2005, I finally found a set of design patterns that came close to what I thinking. One was called *Pedestal*, and that fit with the classical *Adapter* pattern from the original *Design Patterns* book.

I finally understood (after 9 years!) that the "facets" of the hexagon were "ports" through which the system would talk to the outside world, each port being an API that supported a particular conversation with an external agent or actor.

Here is my note on my RSS feed, on July 15, 2005

<item><pubDate>2005 07 15 13:01 MST</pubDate>
<title>

Ports and Adapters Architecture (formerly "Hexagonal" architecture)

</title> <link>

http://c2.com/cgi/wiki?PortsAndAdaptersArchitecture

</link><description>

Somewhere in the mid-90s I started drawing a symmetric architecture in which the database is considered not at the "bottom of the stack", but fully outside the application, just as we recommend doing with the user interface.

To break up perceptions about top and bottom and left and right, I drew it with a hexagonal shape, and came up with the rather lame name HexagonalArchitecture --- simply because I could not identify think of what the "hexagon" meant, but knew it had to have facets, and no number smaller than 5 made visual sense (and pentagons are harder to draw than hexagons).

Finally just worked out what the drawing meant and realized this picture or architecture should be called Ports and Adapters (think operating system or hi-fi ports, and Design Pattern "adapters").

I'll get around to writing a full article on it when I have more examples and project implications to relate, but for now I'm just posting to Ward's wikiwiki site. If you know of prior or related architectural patterns similar to this, write me.

</description>
</item>

In September of 2005, I finally wrote the article describing the pattern, "Ports & Adapters", also known as "Hexagonal Architecture." Hexagonal Architecture is easier to say and remember, so that nickname will always stick, even though the better name is Ports & Adapters.

In this book, we will use the two interchangeably. We will use the name Ports & Adapters when it is really important that we pay attention to the core concepts of the pattern, the ports and the adapters, as opposed to just talking about the pattern in general.

The article, reprinted in full in the next section, is available at [https://alistair.cockburn.us/hexagonal-architecture/].

2017: Juan discovers the pattern

Juan wrote that in 2017,

"I was preparing a medium-large sized application. One day, looking at the screen of my laptop, I realized that it was full of framework code that didn't let me understand what it did regarding business logic. From that moment I began to search the internet and I discovered the architecture that decouples the business logic from the frameworks, and then I also heard of DDD."

He continued:

"From these architectures, the one I liked the most was Hexagonal Architecture, because the mechanism of ports-adapters to communicate is more flexible. That's how I discovered HA. From that moment on until nowadays (and i hope that in the future too) I haven't stopped reading and learning about this pattern."

2017: The Paris talk

Alistair gives his first public talk on the pattern in Paris, with Thomas Pierrain as live programmer for the sample. He creates the terms "driving" and "driven" to refer to the left and right sides, naming the ports with the "for doing something" format.

The pattern was generally ignored until the Domain-Driven Design community started using it. Following that, many people started giving talks and tutorials on the pattern, and getting it generally messed up. Strangely, none of these people ever asked me to look at their interpretations. So in 2015, I asked to give a talk describing the history, intention and structure of the pattern.

Thomas Pierrain was the perfect programmer to program our example live in front of an audience. Things always go wrong in live programming, and sure enough, the entire display projection system failed! It came back on in time for the actual programming.

Thomas called it "Alistair in the Hexagone" (with a gentle reference to the shape of France as a hexagon).

You can see the 3-part sequence, filmed by an attendee in the first row:

Alistair's talk at the flipchart:
https://www.youtube.com/watch?v=th4AgBcrEHA
The two videos with Thomas programming:
https://www.youtube.com/watch?v=iALcE8BPs94
https://www.youtube.com/watch?v=DAe0Bmcyt-4

This talk was when I introduced the "Configurable Dependency" design pattern, which became "Configurable Receiver" after more discussion.

It was also the first time I separated the concepts of *repository* versus *recipient* as secondary or driven actors. They are slightly different when making the architectural drawing, but now we just use the term "driven actor" for either. Although that distinction was to me at the time, is not important any more.

2018: First Spanish version, from Juan Manuel Garrido de Paz

Juan translates into Spanish the pattern and publishes the translation on June 24 in his web site.

https://jmgarridopaz.github.io/content/arquitecturahexagonal.html

2021: Alistair and Juan correct the ambiguous sentence

October 9, 2021: Alistair and Juan together re-wrote one of the sentences in the original, which led to misunderstandings regarding adapters and ports in the driving side.

(Note from Alistair: This shows how dedicated Juan was to correctness. I regard it as a minor miracle that this was the only erroneous sentence he found in all those years of working with that article.)

2022: Component plus Strategy

Alistair finally discovers the UML constructs of *component* and *required interface*, which Juan has pointed to years before. Thus the pattern *Ports & Adapters* becomes a special case of *Component plus Strategy*.

Watching people make a mess of the pattern over the next years bothered me: hexagons within hexagons, several layers deep, hexagons randomly placed in architectural drawings -- none of these solved the problems the pattern addresses.

Finally, in 2022, Juan helped me to understand that the hexagon is properly a Component in the ordinary sense and also according to the UML definition.

A component is something that we understand from ordinary usage, that you can cut out of one place and drop into another place. In order to do that, it has to have well defined APIs on all sides, which is exactly what Hexagonal Architecture calls for.

To make Hexagonal Architecture work properly, though, you need to pass in the handle for the driven actors, something not required by Component.

After some more study, I wrote the article, "Component + Strategy generalizes Ports & Adapters" in 2022.

Here, finally, we see how the Ports & Adapters architecture fits into the UML and patterns literature. A Ports & Adapters implementation is a component with the boundaries set at the technology boundaries (*there are some small variants we will describe later), and with the driven adapters passed in as Strategy objects.

This is described in full in the article, which is included in full in the next section. The article is online at [https://alistaircockburn.com/Articles/Component-Strategy-generalizes-Ports-Adapters].

2023: Configurable Receiver

Alistair and Juan debate the flaws with *dependency injection* and *configurable dependency*. Dan North suggests *configurable receiver*, which Alistair and Juan adopt. The pattern article *Configurable Receiver* is written to put it into the literature.

Around 2010, Gerard Meszaros helped me name a pattern I had struggled with for years: *Configurable Dependency*. I sketched it on my website but never wrote it out. As it is a key concept in the *Ports & Adapters* pattern, it needed to be fleshed out fully.

In 2023, after trying numerous times to define the pattern, Dan North said that the real name of the pattern was *Configurable Receiver*. We decided his name was the correct one and changed our vocabulary. I wrote the pattern finally in May, 2023, see [https://alistaircockburn.com/Articles/Configurable-Receiver].

Reflections on the history

I find it quite frankly astonishing that it has taken me almost 30 years to get to a comfortable place with this pattern, from the first official hexagonal drawing in 1994 to the Component + Strategy article in 2022, to Configurable Receiver in 2023. Who knows, perhaps I'm not there yet.

The pattern is so simple: Just put an API all around your app or system and pass in an argument to set up each secondary connection. Nothing more.

For all that, it is has been difficult to understand and place in the literature of patterns and architectures. Juan and I hope that with this book, the simplicity and the power of the pattern will shine through.

Here is the "thumbnail," or short phrasing of the pattern:

> *Create your application to work without either a UI or a database so you can run automated regression-tests against the application, work when the database becomes unavailable, upgrade to new technology, protect against business logic leaks, and link applications together without any user involvement.*

It is a problem we face often enough: We design a system with particular external technical connections, such as databases and networks, and then one day there is a need to change or take the external technology off-line.

At that moment, development and testing of the system comes to a screeching halt, since everyone is depending on that external technology.

Most development teams simply assume that this scenario won't happen, and just suffer through it when it does happen, as our team had to do in that 1994 project. The cost to protect against this scenario is so low compared to the cost of the delay that there is no good reason not to protect the system from it.

Once that protection is put into place, two more benefits immediately accrue:

* The system is open to having system regression tests for all its functions, from end to end.

* Those external technologies can be varied as technology evolves (as it always does) without enormous effort.

These two additional benefits easily outweigh the small additional cost for implementing the solution. People defend the use of this pattern for any of the above reasons.

How do you get these benefits and set this up? There are 3 steps:

1. Make all services provided by your app, including those used by the UI, available from the system via function calls (the system API, its "provided interface").

2. Add one variable for each of the system's external connections (the 'back-end' actors of the system, so to speak).

3. At system construction or configuration time, pass in to each of those variables the actual external actor or an adapter that can talk to it. Let all calls to those actors go through those variables. These are called the "required interfaces."

The added complexity cost to the system is the addition of those few variables, the configuration code, and the added level of indirection to the external calls.

The system is now completely cut off from the outside world.

It can be tested in isolation through test drivers and mock databases and networks, all under control of the development and test teams.

When some external technology fails, the team can still use the test frameworks to develop and test with.

When technologies change, only a new adapter has to be plugged in for that new technology.

Business logic and external technology code are formally separated and protected from each other.

The cost of bringing in new technologies is vastly lower than it otherwise would be, while the cost of the original implementation is only slightly higher than without the pattern.

In terms of the language used in this book, we say that the system communicates with the outside world through "ports", where a port is an intention or a purpose of a set of interactions. By convention, we name ports for those intentions: "for_calculating_taxes" or "for_getting_tax_rates." In terms of the UML definition of a component, "ports allow you to group the provided and required interfaces into logical interactions that a component has with the outside world."

Naming ports for the intention allows us to collect together all the function calls and protocols around one purpose, and do so without reference to any of the technologies, so that when they change, the port itself does not change.

The things that drive the system we call primary actors or driving actors or just the drivers. The external connections we call secondary actors or driven actors or just the drivens.

The API to the driving actors is what is called in UML the provided interface. It provides the calls that driving actors can use to drive the application. The API toward the external connections is called in UML the required interface. All driven actors must answer to those calls.

With these few elements in place, the app is now cut off from the rest of the world, it has become a component, in the sense of UML.

In practice, we plug this component into the production system by passing the actual adapters to the production repositories and recipients, the driven actors in to those reserved variables. Similarly, we connect this component to whatever driving actors are needed through the setup procedure, and then the entire system is set for production use.

In a testing scenario, we would pass in test doubles for the driven actors and use a test driver with test cases.

That is really all there is to this pattern. All the rest of the pages in this book only expand on this description, trying to anticipate and answer your questions.

6.2. The original article: The Hexagonal (Ports & Adapters) Architecture

Here is the article that kicked it off in 2005. Following the article, we add some comments about the article.

The Hexagonal (Ports & Adapters) Architecture

HaT Technical Report 2005.02
Date: 2005-09-04
Alistair Cockburn

Create your application to work without either a UI or a database so you can run automated regression-tests against the application, work when the database becomes unavailable, and link applications together without any user involvement.

The Pattern: Ports & Adapters (*Object Structural*)

Alternative name: Hexagonal Architecture

Intent

Allow an application to equally be driven by users, programs, automated test or batch scripts, and to be developed and tested in isolation from its eventual run-time devices and databases.

As events arrive from the outside world at a port, a technology-specific adapter converts it into a usable procedure call or message and passes it to the application. The application is blissfully ignorant of the nature of the input device. When the application has something to send out, it sends it out through a port to an adapter, which creates the appropriate signals needed by the receiving technology (human or automated). The application has a semantically sound interaction with the adapters on all sides of it, without actually knowing the nature of the things on the other side of the adapters.

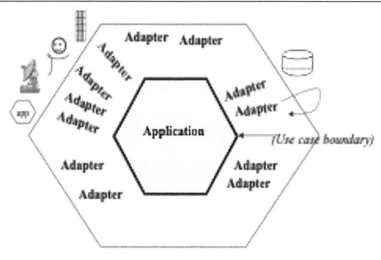

Figure 6.3

Motivation

One of the great bugaboos of software applications over the years has been infiltration of business logic into the user interface code. The problem this causes is threefold: First, the system can't neatly be tested with automated test suites because part of the logic needing to be tested is dependent on oft-changing visual details such as field size and button placement; For the exact same reason, it becomes impossible to shift from a human-driven use of the system to a batch-run system; For still the same reason, it becomes difficult or impossible to allow the program to be driven by another program when that becomes attractive.

The attempted solution, repeated in many organizations, is to create a new layer in the architecture, with the promise that this time, really and truly, no business logic will be put into the new layer. However, having no mechanism to detect when a violation of that promise occurs, the organization finds a few years later that the new layer is cluttered with business logic and the old problem has reappeared.

Imagine now that *every* piece of functionality the application offers were available through an API (application programmed interface) or function call. In this situation, the test or QA department can run automated test scripts against the application to detect when any new coding breaks a previously working function. The business experts can create automated test cases, before the GUI details are finalized, that tells the programmers when they have done their work correctly (and these tests become the ones run by the test department). The application can be deployed in *headless* mode, so only the API is available, and other programs can make use of its functionality -- this simplifies the overall design of complex application suites and also permits business-to-business service applications to use each other without human intervention over the web. Finally, the automated function regression tests detect any violation of the promise to keep business logic out of the presentation layer. The organization can detect, and then correct, the logic leak.

An interesting similar problem exists on what is normally considered "the other side" of the application, where the application logic gets tied to an external database or other service. When the database server goes down or undergoes significant rework or replacement, the programmers can't work because their work is tied to the presence of the database. This causes delay costs and often bad feelings between the people.

It is not obvious that the two problems are related, but there is a symmetry between them that shows up in the nature of the solution.

Nature of the Solution

Both the user-side and the server-side problems actually are caused by the same error in design and programming -- the entanglement between the business logic and the interaction with external entities. The asymmetry to exploit is not that between *left* and *right* sides of the application but between *inside* and *outside* of the application. The rule to obey is that code pertaining to the *inside* part should not leak into the *outside* part.

Removing any left-right or up-down asymmetry for a moment, we see that the application communicates over *ports* to external agencies. The word "port" is supposed to evoke thoughts of *ports* in an operating system, where any device that adheres to the protocols of a port can be plugged into it; and *ports* on electronics gadgets, where again, any device that fits the mechanical and electrical protocols can be plugged in. The protocol for a port is given by the purpose of the conversation between the two devices. The protocol takes the form of an application program interface (API).

For each external device there is an *adapter* that converts the API definition to the signals needed by that device and vice versa. A graphical user interface or GUI is an example of an adapter that maps the movements of a person to the API of the port. Other adapters that fit the same port are automated test harnesses such as FIT or Fitnesse, batch drivers, and any code needed for communication between applications across the enterprise or net.

On another side of the application, the application communicates with an external entity to get data. The protocol is typically a database protocol. From the application's perspective, if the database is moved from a SQL database to a flat file or any other kind of database, the conversation across the API should not change. Additional adapters for the same port thus include an SQL adapter, a flat file adapter, and most importantly, an adapter to a "mock" database, one that sits in memory and doesn't depend on the presence of the real database at all.

Many applications have only two ports: the user-side dialog and the database-side dialog. This gives them an asymmetric appearance, which makes it seem natural to build the application in a one-dimensional, three-, four-, or five-layer stacked architecture.

There are two problems with these drawings. First and worst, people tend not to take the "lines" in the layered drawing seriously. They let the application logic leak across the layer boundaries, causing the problems mentioned above. Secondly, there may be more than two ports to the application, so that the architecture does not fit into the one-dimensional layer drawing.

The hexagonal, or Ports & Adapters, architecture solves these problems by noting the symmetry in the situation: there is an application on the inside communicating over some number of ports with things on the outside. The items outside the application can be dealt with symmetrically.

The hexagon is intended to visually highlight

* the inside-outside asymmetry and the similar nature of ports, to get away from the one-dimensional layered picture and all that evokes, and

* the presence of a defined number of different ports - two, three, or four (four is most I have encountered to date).

The hexagon is not a hexagon because the number six is important, but rather to allow the people doing the drawing to have room to insert Ports & Adapters as they need, not being constrained by a one-dimensional layered drawing. The term *hexagonal architecture* comes from this visual effect.

The term "port and adapters" picks up the *purposes* of the parts of the drawing. A port identifies a purposeful conversation. There will typically be multiple adapters for any one port, for various technologies that may plug into that port. Typically, these might include a phone answering machine, a human voice, a touch-tone phone, a graphical human interface, a test harness, a batch driver, an http interface, a direct program-to-program interface, a mock (in-memory) database, a real database (perhaps different databases for development, test, and real use).

In the Application Notes, the left-right asymmetry will be brought up again. However, the primary purpose of this pattern is to focus on the inside-outside asymmetry, pretending briefly that all external items are identical from the perspective of the application.

Structure

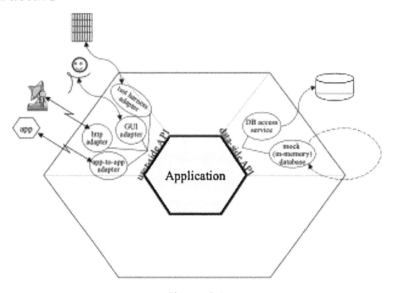

Figure 6.4

Figure 6.4 shows an application having two active ports and several adapters for each port. The two ports are the application-controlling side and the data-retrieval side. This drawing shows that the application can be equally driven by an automated, system-level regression test suite, by a human user, by a remote http application, or by another local application. On the data side, the application can be configured to run decoupled from external databases using an in-memory oracle, or mock, database replacement; or it can run against the test- or run-time database. The functional specification of the application, perhaps in use cases, is made against the inner hexagon's interface and not against any one of the external technologies that might be used.

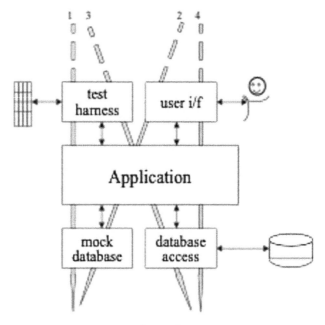

Figure 6.5

Figure 6.5 shows the same application mapped to a three-layer architectural drawing. To simplify the drawing only two adapters are shown for each port. This drawing is intended to show how multiple adapters fit in the top and bottom layers, and the sequence in which the various adapters are used during system development. The numbered arrows show the order in which a team might develop and use the application:

1. With a FIT test harness driving the application and using the mock (in-memory) database substituting for the real database;

2. Adding a GUI to the application, still running off the mock database;

3. In integration testing, with automated test scripts (e.g., from Cruise Control) driving the application against a real database containing test data;

4. In real use, with a person using the application to access a live database.

Sample Code

The simplest application that demonstrates the Ports & Adapters architecture fortunately comes with the FIT documentation. It is a simple discount computing application:

discount(amount) = amount * rate(amount);

In our adaptation, the amount will come from the user and the rate will come from a database, so there will be two ports. We implement them in stages:

* With tests but with a constant rate instead of a mock database,

* then with the GUI,

* then with a mock database that can be swapped out for a real database.

Thanks to Gyan Sharma at IHC for providing the code for this example.

Stage 1: FIT + App + constant-as-mock-database

First we create the test cases as an HTML table (see the FIT documentation for this):

TestDiscounter	
amount	discount()
100	5
200	10

Note that the column names will become class and function names in our program. FIT contains ways to get rid of this "programmerese", but for this article it is easier just to leave them in.

Knowing what the test data will be, we create the user-side adapter, the ColumnFixture that comes with FIT as shipped:

```
import fit.ColumnFixture;
public class TestDiscounter extends ColumnFixture
{
   private Discounter app = new Discounter();
   public double amount;
   public double discount() {    return app.discount(amount);  }}
```

That's actually all there is to the adapter. So far, the tests run from the command line (see the FIT book for the path you'll need). We used this one:

```
set FIT_HOME=/FIT/FitLibraryForFit15Feb2005
java
    -cp
%FIT_HOME%/lib/javaFit1.1b.jar;%FIT_HOME%/dist/fitLibraryForFit.jar;
src;bin
    fit.FileRunner   test/Discounter.html   TestDiscount_Output.html
```

FIT produces an output file with colors showing us what passed (or failed, in case we made a typo somewhere along the way).

At this point the code is ready to check in, hook into Cruise Control or your automated build machine, and include in the build-and-test suite.

Stage 2: UI + App + constant-as-mock-database

I'm going to let you create your own UI and have it drive the Discounter application, since the code is a bit long to include here. Some of the key lines in the code are these:

```
...
Discounter app = new Discounter();
public void actionPerformed(ActionEvent event) {
   ...String amountStr = text1.getText();
   double amount = Double.parseDouble(amountStr);
   discount = app.discount(amount));
   text3.setText( "" + discount );
   ...
```

At this point the application can be both demoed and regression tested. The user-side adapters are both running.

Stage 3: (FIT or UI) + App + mock database

To create a replaceable adapter for the database side, we create an *interface* to a repository, a *RepositoryFactory* that will produce either the mock database or the real service object, and the in-memory mock for the database.

```
public interface RateRepository {
   double getRate(double amount);
}
```

```
public class RepositoryFactory {
   public RepositoryFactory() { super(); }
   public static RateRepository getMockRateRepository() {
      return new MockRateRepository();
   }
}
```

```
public class MockRateRepository implements RateRepository {
   public double getRate(double amount) {
      if(amount <= 100) return 0.01;
      if(amount <= 1000) return 0.02;
      return 0.05;
   }
}
```

To hook this adapter into the Discounter application, we need to update the application itself to accept a repository adapter to use, and then have the (FIT or UI) user-side adapter pass the repository to use (real or mock) into the constructor of the application itself. Here is the updated application and a FIT adapter that passes in a mock repository (the FIT adapter code to choose whether to pass in the mock or real repository's adapter is longer without adding much new information, so I omit that version here).

```
import repository.RepositoryFactory;
import repository.RateRepository;
public class Discounter {
  private RateRepository rateRepository;
  public Discounter(RateRepository r) {
    super();
    rateRepository = r;
  }
  public double discount(double amount) {
    double rate = rateRepository.getRate( amount );
    return amount * rate;
  }
}
```

```
import app.Discounter;
import fit.ColumnFixture;
public class TestDiscounter extends ColumnFixture {
  private Discounter app =
    new Discounter(RepositoryFactory.getMockRateRepository());
  public double amount;
  public double discount() {
    return app.discount( amount );
  }
}
```

That concludes implementation of the simplest version of the hexagonal architecture.

Application Notes

The Left-Right Asymmetry

The Ports & Adapters pattern is deliberately written pretending that all ports are fundamentally similar. That pretense is useful at the architectural level. In implementation, Ports & Adapters show up in two flavors, which I'll call *primary* and *secondary*, for soon-to-be-obvious reasons. They could be also called *driving* adapters and *driven* adapters.

The alert reader will have noticed that in all the examples given, FIT fixtures are used on the left-side ports and mocks on the right. In the three-layer architecture, FIT sits in the top layer and the mock sits in the bottom layer.

This is related to the idea from use cases of "primary actors" and "secondary actors." A *primary actor* is an actor that drives the application (takes it out of quiescent state to perform one of its advertised functions). A *secondary actor* is one that the application drives, either to get answers from or to merely notify. The distinction between *primary* and *secondary* lies in who triggers or is in charge of the conversation.

The natural test adapter to substitute for a *primary* actor is FIT, since that framework is designed to read a script and drive the application. The natural test adapter to substitute for a *secondary* actor such as a database is a mock, since that is designed to answer queries or record events from the application.

These observations lead us to follow the system's use case context diagram and draw the *primary ports* and *primary adapters* on the left side (or top) of the hexagon, and the *secondary ports* and *secondary adapters* on the right (or bottom) side of the hexagon.

The relationship between primary and secondary ports/adapters and their respective implementation in FIT and mocks is useful to keep in mind, but it should be used as a consequence of using the Ports & Adapters architecture, not to short-circuit it. The ultimate benefit of a Ports & Adapters implementation is the ability to run the application in a fully isolated mode.

Use Cases And The Application Boundary

It is useful to use the hexagonal architecture pattern to reinforce the preferred way of writing use cases.

A common mistake is to write use cases to contain intimate knowledge of the technology sitting outside each port. These use cases have earned a justifiably bad name in the industry for being long, hard-to-read, boring, brittle, and expensive to maintain.

Understanding the Ports & Adapters architecture, we can see that the use cases should generally be written at the application boundary (the inner hexagon), to specify the functions and events supported by the application, regardless of external technology. These use cases are shorter, easier to read, less expensive to maintain, and more stable over time.

How Many Ports?

What exactly a port is and isn't is largely a matter of taste. At the one extreme, every use case could be given its own port, producing hundreds of ports for many applications. Alternatively, one could imagine merging all primary ports and all secondary ports so there are only two ports, a left side and a right side.

Neither extreme appears optimal.

The weather system described in the Known Uses has four natural ports: the weather feed, the administrator, the notified subscribers, the subscriber database. A coffee machine controller has four natural ports: the user, the database containing the recipes and prices, the dispensers, and the coin box. A hospital medication system might have three: one for the nurse, one for the prescription database, and one for the computer-controller medication dispensers.

It doesn't appear that there is any particular damage in choosing the "wrong" number of ports, so that remains a matter of intuition. My selection tends to favor a small number, two, three or four ports, as described above and in the Known Uses.

Known Uses

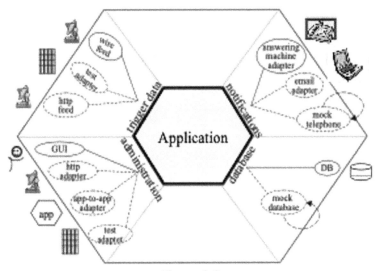

Figure 6.6

Figure 6.6 shows an application with four ports and several adapters at each port. This was derived from an application that listened for alerts from the national weather service about earthquakes, tornadoes, fires and floods, and notified people on their telephones or telephone answering machines. At the time we discussed this system, the system's interfaces were identified and discussed by *technology, linked to purpose*. There was an interface for trigger-data arriving over a wire feed, one for notification data to be sent to answering machines, an administrative interface implemented in a GUI, and a database interface to get their subscriber data.

The people were struggling because they needed to add an http interface from the weather service, an email interface to their subscribers, and they had to find a way to bundle and unbundle their growing application suite for different customer purchasing preferences. They feared they were staring at a maintenance and testing nightmare as they had to implement, test and maintain separate versions for all combinations and permutations.

Their shift in design was to architect the system's interfaces *by purpose* rather than by technology, and to have the technologies be substitutable (on all sides) by adapters. They immediately picked up the ability to include the http feed and the email notification (the new adapters are shown in the drawing with dashed lines). By making each application executable in headless mode through APIs, they could add an app-to-app adapter and unbundle the application suite, connecting the sub-applications on demand. Finally, by making each application executable completely in isolation, with test and mock adapters in place, they gained the ability to regression test their applications with stand-alone automated test scripts.

Mac, Windows, Google, Flickr, Web 2.0

In the early 1990s, MacIntosh applications such as word processor applications were required to have API-drivable interfaces, so that applications and user-written scripts could access all the functions of the applications. Windows desktop applications have evolved the same ability (I don't have the historical knowledge to say which came first, nor is that relevant to the point).

The current (2005) trend in web applications is to publish an API and let other web applications access those APIs directly. Thus, it is possible to publish local crime data over a Google map, or create web applications that include Flickr's photo archiving and annotating abilities.

All of these examples are about making the *primary* ports' APIs visible. We see no information here about the secondary ports.

Stored Outputs

This example written by Willem Bogaerts on the C2 wiki:

"I encountered something similar, but mainly because my application layer had a strong tendency to become a telephone switchboard that managed things it should not do. My application generated output, showed it to the user and then had some possibility to store it as well. My main problem was that you did not need to store it always. So my application generated output, had to buffer it and present it to the user. Then, when the user decided that he wanted to store the output, the application retrieved the buffer and stored it for real.

I did not like this at all. Then I came up with a solution: Have a presentation control with storage facilities. Now the application no longer channels the output in different directions, but it simply outputs it to the presentation control. It's the presentation control that buffers the answer and gives the user the possibility to store it.

The traditional layered architecture stresses "UI" and "storage" to be different. The Ports & Adapters Architecture can reduce output to being simply "output" again."

Anonymous example from the C2 wiki

"In one project I worked on, we used the SystemMetaphor of a component stereo system. Each component has defined interfaces, each of which has a specific purpose. We can then connect components together in almost unlimited ways using simple cables and adapters."

Distributed, Large-Team Development

This one is still in trial use and so does not properly count as a use of the pattern. However, it is interesting to consider.

Teams in different locations all build to the Hexagonal architecture, using FIT and mocks so the applications or components can be tested in standalone mode. The CruiseControl build runs every half hour and runs all the applications using the FIT+mock combination. As application subsystem and databases get completed, the mocks are replaced with test databases.

Separating Development of UI & Application Logic

This one is still in early trial use and so does not count as a use of the pattern. However, it is interesting to consider.

The UI design is unstable, as they haven't decided on a driving technology or a metaphor yet. The back-end services architecture hasn't been decided, and in fact will probably change several times over the next six months. Nonetheless, the project has officially started and time is ticking by.

The application team creates FIT tests and mocks to isolate their application, and creates testable, demonstrable functionality to show their users. When the UI and back-end services decisions finally get met, it "should be straightforward" to add those elements the application. Stay tuned to learn how this works out (or try it yourself and write me to let me know).

Related Patterns

Adapter

The *Design Patterns* book contains a description of the generic *Adapter* pattern: "Convert the interface of a class into another interface clients expect." The ports-and-adapters pattern is a particular use of the *Adapter* pattern.

Model-View-Controller

The MVC pattern was implemented as early as 1974 in the Smalltalk project. It has been given, over the early, many variations, such as Model-Interactor and Model-View-Presenter. Each of these implements the idea of ports-and-adapters on the primary ports, not the secondary ports.

Mock Objects and Loopback

"A mock object is a "double agent" used to test the behaviour of other objects. First, a mock object acts as a faux implementation of an interface or class that mimics the external behaviour of a true implementation. Second, a mock object observes how other objects interact with its methods and compares actual behaviour with preset expectations. When a discrepancy occurs, a mock object can interrupt the test and report the anomaly. If the discrepancy cannot be noted during the test, a verification method called by the tester ensures that all expectations have been met or failures reported." -- From http://MockObjects.com

Fully implemented according to the mock-object agenda, mock objects are used throughout an application, not just at the external interface. The primary thrust of the mock object movement is conformance to specified protocol at the individual class and object level. I borrow their word "mock" as the best short description of an in-memory substitute for an external secondary actor.

The Loopback pattern is an explicit pattern for creating an internal replacement for an external device.

Pedestals

In "Patterns for Generating a Layered Architecture", Barry Rubel describes a pattern about creating an axis of symmetry in control software that is very similar to Ports & Adapters. The *Pedestal* pattern calls for implementing an object representing each hardware device within the system, and linking those objects together in a control layer. The *Pedestal* pattern can be used to describe either side of the hexagonal architecture, but does not yet stress the similarity across adapters. Also, being written for a mechanical control environment, it is not so easy to see how to apply the pattern to IT applications.

Checks

Ward Cunningham's pattern language for detecting and handling user input errors, is good for error handling across the inner hexagon boundaries.

Dependency Inversion, Dependency Injection and SPRING

Bob Martin's Dependency Inversion Principle states that "High-level modules should not depend on low-level modules. Both should depend on abstractions. Abstractions should not depend on details. Details should depend on abstractions." The *Dependency Injection* pattern by Martin Fowler gives some implementations. These show how to create swappable secondary actor adapters. The code can be typed in directly, as done in the sample code in the article, or using configuration files and having the SPRING framework generate the equivalent code.

Acknowledgements

Thanks to Gyan Sharma at Intermountain Health Care for providing the sample code used here. Thanks to Rebecca Wirfs-Brock for her book *Object Design*, which when read together with the *Adapter* pattern from the *Design Patterns* book, helped me to understand what the hexagon was about. Thanks also to the people on Ward's wiki, who provided comments about this pattern over the years (e.g., particularly Kevin Rutherfold's http://silkandspinach.net/blog/2004/07/hexagonal_soup.html).

References and Related Reading

FIT, A Framework for Integrating Testing: Cunningham, W., online at http://fit.c2.com, and Mugridge, R. and Cunningham, W., *Fit for Developing Software*, Prentice-Hall PTR, 2005.

The *Adapter* pattern: in Gamma, E., Helm, R., Johnson, R., Vlissides, J., *Design Patterns*, Addison-Wesley, 1995, pp. 139-150.

The *Pedestal* pattern: in Rubel, B., "Patterns for Generating a Layered Architecture", in Coplien, J., Schmidt, D., *PatternLanguages of Program Design*, Addison-Wesley, 1995, pp. 119-150.

The *Checks* pattern: by Cunningham, W., online at http://c2.com/ppr/checks.html

The *Dependency Inversion Principle*: Martin, R., in *Agile Software Development Principles Patterns and Practices*, Prentice Hall, 2003, Chapter 11: "The Dependency-Inversion Principle", and online at http://www.objectmentor.com/resources/articles/dip.pdf

The *Dependency Injection* pattern: Fowler, M., online at http://www.martinfowler.com/articles/injection.html

The *Mock Object* pattern: Freeman, S. online at http://MockObjects.com

The *Loopback* pattern: Cockburn, A., online at http://c2.com/cgi/wiki?LoopBack

Use cases: Cockburn, A., *Writing Effective Use Cases*, Addison-Wesley, 2001, and Cockburn, A., "Structuring Use Cases with Goals", online at http://alistair.cockburn.us/crystal/articles/sucwg/structuringucswithgoals.htm

6.3. Comments on the original article in 2023

The article has held up quite well. A few people found one sentence confusing and possibly incorrect:

> "As events arrive from the outside world at a port, a technology-specific adapter converts it into a usable procedure call or message and passes it to the application."

Alistair updated that on the web to read:

> "When any driver wants to use the application at a port, it sends a request that is converted by an adapter for the specific technology of the driver into a usable procedure call or message, which passes that to the application port."

Actually, that's still a bit misleading.

Sometimes a driving actor needs an adapter, sometimes it doesn't. The pattern doesn't distinguish or care about this, all that happens *outside* the application. We suffered from not having a word that means "the driver if it doesn't need an adapter or the adapter for the driver if that is needed", so we added the word "interactor" to mean that.

From the point of view of the pattern, all of this is *outside* the app. Events show up at a port. You may or may not need an adapter for any given driver.

6.4. The article: "Component + Strategy generalizes Ports & Adapters"

In 2022, Alistair published a follow-up article recognizing that the Ports & Adapters architecture is really just a special application of the UML "Component" element placed at the technology boundaries of a system, and configured via "Strategy" objects passed in to the component.

Here is that article, unretouched:

Component-plus-Strategy generalizes Ports-and-Adapters

Alistair Cockburn
Humans and Technology Technical Report 2022.01 (v3a, 2023-06-01)
© Alistair Cockburn, 2022 all rights reserved

Component + Strategy allows you to configure a subsystem to fit into slightly different environments. *Hexagonal Architecture* aka *Ports & Adapters* is a specific version of it that allows you to isolate a system from external technologies, vary those external technologies, and test the system in isolation from those technologies.

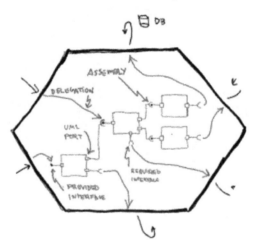

Figure 6.7

Table of Contents:

Warmup:

You quite naturally pass an object into a function so that the function can ask that object for more information or tell it to do something. This is normal object-oriented design.

For example, suppose you are programming a coffee machine that operates from recipes, you might pass in a recipe object to the drink-maker, so that the drink maker can get from it the sequence of ingredients to dispense.

Your code would look something like:

```
recipe = RecipeLibrary.find( "mochaccino" );
drinkmaker.make( recipe )
```

and inside the drinkmaker:

```
foreach step in recipe {
    dispenser = step.ingredient
    quantity - step.quantity
    dispenser.dispense( quantity )
}
```

Figure 6.8: The inevitable coffee machine

Although this is all really normal, it turns out to be quite subtle. It has been written about a lot, and given lots of fancy names.

First of all, we have **parameterized the recipes**, meaning, we choose which one to use according to the argument we pass in to the function. This is a really basic way to program, and should be fairly understandable. The main reason I mention it is that I want to be able to say in a bit: "parameterize the secondary actors." All I mean with that is that you pass in an argument that identifies which one to use.

It turns out we have just implemented the *Strategy* pattern. Many programmers don't use *Strategy* consciously, because it seems complicated in the *Design Patterns* book. So although they might use it reflexively, they don't describe their designs this way.

The Strategy pattern, very briefly, looks like this:

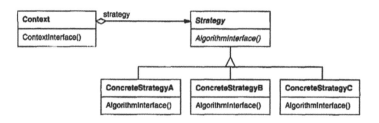

Figure 6.9: The *Strategy* pattern

The *Strategy* pattern only says that an object ("Context" here) has in its hands one of a set of possible objects that all respond to the same function call. Pretty ordinary polymorphism going on there.

In this drawing, the diagram shows the concrete strategies as *subclasses* of the top strategy class. But that only is needed in some languages. In languages such as Ruby, Smalltalk, and others, the concrete strategies only have to meet the function call interface, there is no need for an abstract superclass over them. This becomes important later.

What's cool about *Strategy* is that that polymorphism not only saves a bunch of 'if' statements, but the Context doesn't know or care which it has at the time of the call.

Context may have calculated which one it needed earlier - for example, it may earlier have decided to use a time-optimal search or a space-optimal search, and obtained the appropriate search algorithm from somewhere, stuffed that search algorithm object into a safe place, and when needed, invoked whatever it had stored away.

Or, the Context object might never know which concrete strategy object it is calling. Something, somewhere else, made that decision, and passed it in as a parameter. This is what we did with the recipe object.

The *Strategy* pattern doesn't tell us how the concrete strategy got loaded into the Context object. That is outside the scope of the pattern. As we discuss patterns in this article, we will pay attention to this - what does the pattern legislate versus which is outside the scope of the pattern.

Thirdly, we have just used what is known in UML as a **Required Interface**. The drinkmaker declares what calls it will make to its argument-collaborators, and they have to implement that. This is exactly what the *Strategy* pattern shows, above, although it is not evident to the casual reader that that is what is going on.

But we're not done with the example, yet. It also turns out that we have implemented the *Dependency Injection* pattern, one of the implementation possibilities of **Configurable Receiver** [https://alistaircockburn.com/Articles/Configurable-Receiver].

Wait! What?!

Let's draw a picture of the drinkmaker using UML notation.

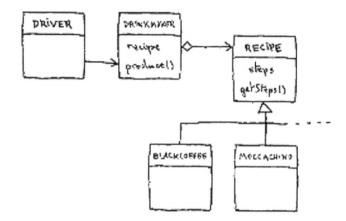

Figure 6.10: The drinkmaker example
(Image courtesy of Juan Manuel Garrido de Paz)

The simple arrowheads show a calling, or *uses* relation of the driver to the drinkmaker. The driver selects the recipe and passes it to the drinkmaker using what UML calls the drinkmaker's **Provided Interface.**

The open triangle shows an *implements* relation. Each recipe must implement the **Required Interface** of the drinkmaker. These are the same two arrowheads as in the *Strategy* diagram, except that the Strategy diagram does not show an outer driver calling the Context object, because that is out of scope of the pattern.

Because driver passes the recipe into the drinkmaker, the drinkmaker knows nothing about those other objects at programming time. It has no code-level dependencies on them. All knowledge it needs it obtains as needed during program execution. We like this, from a maintenance, testing, and reuse perspective.

To end this warmup section, what I am wanting to show here is how normal it is to pass an object as an argument to a function for further investigation, and how that simple act implements all of: **parameterized collaborator, Configurable Receiver, Dependency Injection, Strategy** and **Required Interface.** That's a lot of buzzwords for a fairly normal design practice

*   *   *   *   *

Introducing components and ports

I only just discovered in 2022(!) that UML contains a thing called **Component**, which has a **Provided Interface** or API on the driver side, and a **Required Interface** on the collaborator side. Further, **Component** has a thing called a **Port**, which is just a requirement that anything that plugs into the component must honor a protocol.

The UML spec says a Component is, "a modular unit with well-defined Interfaces that is replaceable within its environment."

"A Component specifies a formal contract of the services that it provides to its clients and those that it requires from other Components or services in the system in terms of its provided and required Interfaces."

Here is the UML picture for a component

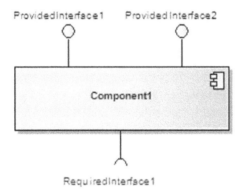

Figure 6.11: A UML Component with Provided and Required interfaces

A key property of components that is relevant to this article is that they can be nested - components inside of components - at any number of levels. This allows you to construct subsystems out of individual components and other subsystems. When we compare this to the *Ports & Adapters* or *Hexagonal Architecture* pattern, which doesn't nest, we will see this as a key difference between the two.

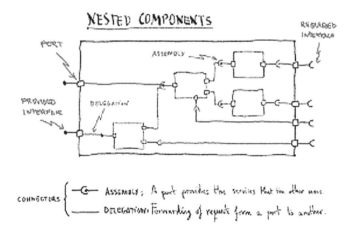

Figure 6.12: Components can be nested
(Image courtesy of Juan Manuel Garrido de Paz)

(formerly: https://www.uml-diagrams.org/component-diagrams/component-diagram-overview.png

Finally, we must note that we have shifted from a pure *modeling* discussion to one that includes *packaging*. The packaging is conceptual at the first hand, because we are asserting that a collection of things has a boundary and specified set of ways to interact with it. It may also be physical, in terms of being a stored or deployable unit.

What we're going to do now is a bit usual, we're going to blend a packaging discussion with a modeling discussion into one pattern. We are going to configure our Component with a Strategy.

But first we have to ask: *Strategy?* or *Adapter?*

*   *   *   *   *

Strategy, Adapter, or both?

The *Adapter* pattern is a special case of the *Strategy* pattern in which the concrete strategy will make some adjustments for interface compatibility and then call another service to take care of the request. The big difference between the two is that *Adapter* has an additional level of indirection. The strategy may or may not do all its work itself, but we intend the adapter to connect to something else.

A *Strategy* object can, of course, do all this - that is outside the pattern definition - but we *expect* the *Adapter* to do this.

Now, I know the names are different, but for a moment I just want to look at the structure of the code, because we'll make use of that.

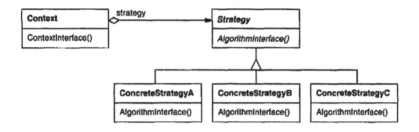

Figure 6-9 repeated: The *Strategy* pattern again

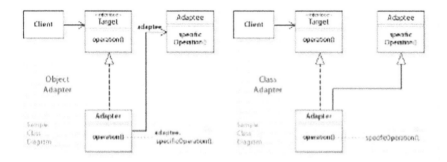

Figure 6.13: The *Adapter* pattern

You might notice that in the diagrams, the *Adapter* picture only shows one adapter, where the *Strategy* picture shows several, we imagine swappable, concrete strategies. But this is only in the drawing. In ordinary working, we are quite likely to send a message out to a web channel, a text message, or something else, and vary that during program execution. So, there are just as likely to be several concrete adapters classes that get called and swapped at program configuration time or run time.

Where this similarity between the patterns this becomes useful is that you can combine Strategies and Adapters. The following example shows them together. The first indicated strategy might do all the work itself, the second uses a third object to complete the work.

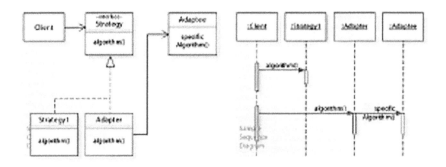

Figure 6.14: Using *Strategy* and *Adapter* together
http://www.w3sdesign.com/GoF_Design_Patterns_Reference0100.pdf

We will make use of this combined pattern in testing our component.

For the above reasons, I call the pattern in this article *Component + Strategy*. I will specialize it to the *Ports & Adapters* or *Hexagonal Architecture* pattern.

*   *   *   *   *

The Pattern: Component + Strategy

Component + Strategy allows you to configure a subsystem to fit into slightly different environments.

Because we have a packaging element connected to a modeling element, I show the pattern in two diagrams, a component diagram with an object hanging off it, and a class diagram showing the component as a single class, even though it probably consists of many.

First, just to get us used to looking at them, here is the *Strategy* pattern shown as a component diagram.

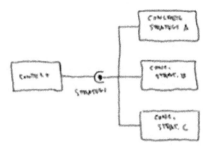

Figure 6.15: *Strategy* as a component diagram
(Image courtesy of Juan Manuel Garrido de Paz)

Next, here is *Component + Strategy* as a component diagram:

Figure 6.16: *Component + Strategy* as a component diagram
(Image courtesy of Juan Manuel Garrido de Paz)

Finally, here is *Component + Strategy* as a class diagram

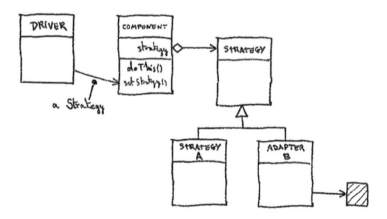

Figure 6.17: *Component + Strategy* as a class diagram
(Image courtesy of Juan Manuel Garrido de Paz)

One of the benefits of using *Component + Strategy* is that by declaring the component boundary explicitly, you can supply a test double as the strategy for one of external actors and thus test the component in isolation. Then for production use, supply an adapter to do the real connection.

And now our Strategy-Adapter discussion becomes relevant. The test double might not be connected to a test database. If it is not, then the test double fits the definition of a *Strategy* object, as we discussed above. If it is connected to a test database, then it is arguably an adapter. Personally, I am not fussed which way you call it, I don't consider that argument worth the time fighting over it. I am only going into this detail here because this is the pattern definition, and I would like to be as accurate as possible with the terms.

In the end, I am choosing the name *Component + Strategy* instead of *Component + Adapter* because *Strategy* is the more general of the two.

*   *   *   *   *

Ports & Adapters (Hexagonal Architecture) revisited

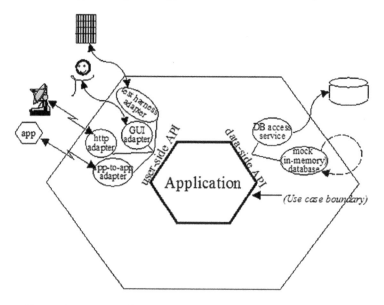

Figure 6.18: Ports & Adapters aka Hexagonal Architecture

Given the above, we can now see that the *Ports & Adapters* also known as *Hexagonal* architecture is a specific use of *Component + Strategy* where the component boundary is placed just in front of external technologies. *Adapter* objects are supplied for each port to adjust to the **Provided Interface** or **Required Interface** of the component.

In the case of direct module-to-module interaction where the interfaces are compatible, no adapter may be needed.

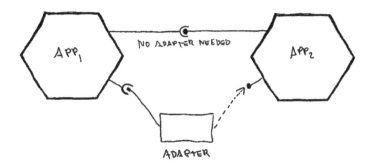

Figure 6.19: *Apps interacting with and without needing adapters*
(Image courtesy of Juan Manuel Garrido de Paz)

In testing, test doubles may be either *Strategy* or *Adapter* objects.

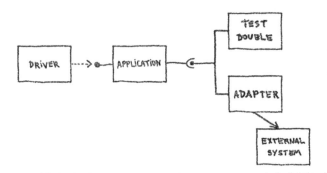

Figure 6.20: *Ports & Adapters* as component diagram showing test double
(Image courtesy of Juan Manuel Garrido de Paz)

One of the differences between the two patterns is that a key intention of *Ports & Adapters* is to protect against external technology changes. Hence, its boundary is placed only at the technology boundary. It is not nestable, unlike *Component + Strategy*, which is designed to be nested.

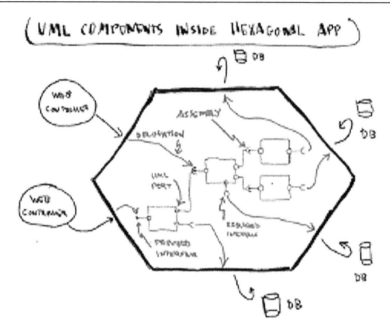

Figure 6.21: *Components* within *Ports & Adapters*
(Image courtesy of Juan Manuel Garrido de Paz)

Testing should be the same for *Ports & Adapters* as for *Component + Strategy*. Place a test driver or test double at each port to test the component in isolation.

For the definition of *Hexagonal Architecture*, see
https://alistair.cockburn.us/hexagonal-architecture/

*   *   *   *   *

The Hidden Fourth Object, the Configurator

All of the preceding diagrams and discussions skipped over an important question:

How do all these objects come to know of each other?

The Strategy diagram doesn't show how the Context object came to know which concrete strategy to use. That is outside the scope of the pattern. The same is true for both Component + Strategy and Ports & Adapters.

However, sooner or later there has to be some module or code that knows all the players and introduces them to each other. That's where source-code dependencies lie. This is the Configurator object. There are a few other solutions, but this one is the most common.

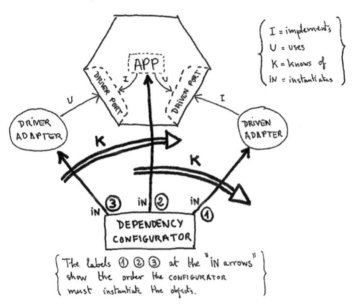

Figure 6.22: The Configurator sets up the knowledge paths
(Image courtesy of Juan Manuel Garrido de Paz)

When you test at the system level, there is no UI and there are no databases. You have a test harness driving the Provided Interface, and a test double handling the requests at the Required Interface.

You write a module where you instantiate all three of them: the test harness, the test double, and the component, you tell the test harness to use the component, and send the test double in to the component as the concrete strategy at the Required Interface. Then you tell the test harness to go, and it all runs.

In early stages of development, each test case does all that wiring and then runs the specific test. Here, the configurator is inside each test case.

Then, for production use, all those same instantiations take place in the program build and startup. The startup module will instantiate the component, the UI, and the adapters to the relevant databases and other actors. Depending on your design, the configurator may pass in the strategy objects to the component or that may be the assignment for the UI or another module. In all cases, the configurator knows all the players and what they need.

Because the Configurator is outside the pattern definition - exactly how and where all that knowledge acquisition happens - we generally don't see the Configurator getting talked about. In order to make the patterns useful, though, we need to make it explicit.

For completeness, Juan Manuel Garrido de Paz was kind enough to contribute this Spring code that illustrates:

```
@Configuration
public class SpringDiscounterAppConfigurator {

    @Bean
    @ConditionalOnProperty(name = "for-managing-discounts", havingValue
= "test-cases")
    public Driver testCasesDriver ( ForDiscounting discounterApp ) {
        return new TestCases( discounterApp );
    }

    @Bean
    @ConditionalOnProperty(name = "for-managing-discounts", havingValue
= "cli")
    public Driver cliDriver ( ForDiscounting discounterApp ) {
        return new Console(discounterApp);
    }

    @Bean
    public ForDiscounting discounterApp (ForObtainingRates rateRepository )
```

```
{
    return new DiscounterApp ( rateRepository );
  }

  @Bean
  @ConditionalOnProperty(name = "for-obtaining-rates", havingValue =
"test-double")
  public ForObtainingRates testDoubleRateRepository() {
    return new StubRateRepository();
  }

  @Bean
  @ConditionalOnProperty(name = "for-obtaining-rates", havingValue =
"file")
  public ForObtainingRates fileRateRepository() {
    return new FileRateRepository();
  }

}
```

*   *   *   *   *

Tests or no tests?

One of the things that makes my blood freeze when seeing people claim they have implemented *Ports & Adapters* or *Hexagonal Architecture* is the absence of tests on both sides.

If you place hexagons everywhere, at different levels inside the system, then there will be too much repetition between the hexagon boundary tests and the system tests. Not being worth the time to write and maintain both, the team will likely stop writing tests for the inner hexagons, at which point it ceases to be a real Component.

One reason I like UML's *Component* is that simply by using the word 'component', you should feel obligated to write tests at all of the boundaries. I mean, it is called a "component" after all, and is intended to be placed in different systems and circumstances. Of course there should be tests at the declared boundaries.

Perhaps because the *Ports & Adapters Architecture* pattern never explicitly says it is a component, people think of it only as a conceptual interface, a "nice thought", but not really something to write tests at.

My hope is that by writing *Component + Strategy*, and then making it clear that *Ports & Adapters* is a special case of that general pattern, people will start to treat these boundaries as real system boundaries, and hence worth the trouble of writing tests to.

It is for this reason that I am adamant that *Ports & Adapters* aka *Hexagonal Architecture* is placed at the outer, technology boundary. At that interface, the tests are meaningful system tests, worth maintaining. The application becomes a component in the sense we intend, and gets its proper regression tests.

*　*　*　*　*

End Notes

The point of the opening example was to show how simple and ordinary our design was. We simply parameterized an external resource, then passed in an object that let us get the appropriate one at run time.

The difference between *Component + Strategy* and *Ports & Adapters* or *Hexagonal Architecture* is that *Ports & Adapters* is aimed at solving one very specific problem - changing external technologies (and testing) - whereas *Component + Strategy* is intended as a general subsystem-bounding effort.

I would like to see increased use of *Component + Strategy* as a packaging concept that allows arbitrary sub-sections of code to be protected by a test wall and configured to their environments.

6.5. The article: "Configurable Receiver"

Here is the final article in the series, published in 2023.

Configurable Receiver Subsumes Dependency Injection and Dependency Lookup

Alistair Cockburn
Humans and Technology Technical Report 2023.01
(v21c, 2023-06-02)
© Alistair Cockburn, 2023 all rights reserved

The Pattern: Configurable Receiver (*Behavioral*)

Set or alter a receiver at run time.

Arranging for the receiver to be set at run time affects both the source code structure and the run-time behavior. This pattern addresses both.

Configurable Receiver subsumes *Dependency Injection* and *Dependency Lookup*.

1. Motivation and informal structure

Whether functions, objects, or systems, a *sender* needs to call or send a message to a *receiver*. We sometimes want to set the receiver at run time. For example:

To develop a system with test data, then put it into production using production data without having to change the source code, but just to restart the system and set whichever data supplier we need during initialization.

To evolve the system, using perhaps data files to start with and evolving to different databases over time.

To change receivers in real time based on the data being handled.

For the receiver to be configurable at run time, we need to add a configurator (Figure 6.23). The specific design for the configurator is outside the pattern, as will be discussed.

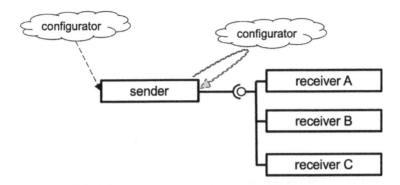

Figure 6.23. Informal view of Configurable Receiver, showing two choices for the placement of the configurator.

2. When to use the pattern

This pattern trades complexity for flexibility. Here, I present that trade using *Indications, Counterindications, Complicating side effects*, and *Overdose effect* (the idea that too much of a good thing is not a good thing).

Indications:

* You want to be able to set the receiver during execution, whether at initialization, in real time per individual data, or over a period of years as technologies shift.

* You want to be able to replace production connections with test harnesses, and back again, without changing the sender's source code.

* In all cases, you want to avoid having to change the source code and then rebuild the system every time you make these shifts.

Counterindications:

* You don't see those things in your future, and you don't want to add complexity to your system unnecessarily.

* Not every receiver of every message needs to be configurable, so you choose the moments at which to implement this pattern.

Complicating Side Effects:

* Since the call will be determined at run time, it adds one more layer of indirection.

* You must introduce a *configurator* that will provide the receiver to the sender, and you will have to walk through all the design choices that surround the configurator.

* Either the sender will have a provided interface for the configurator to pass in the receiver, or the sender makes an extra call to the configurator to get the receiver.

* Either the sender has one more local variable to hold the receiver, or must get the receiver every time.

* In statically type-checked languages, the sender must declare the interface that all intended receivers must implement. (This is not needed in dynamic languages.)

* In those statically type-checked languages, declaring that interface adds complexity to the source code folder structure.

Overdose Effect:

* If you put Configurable Receivers everywhere, your code becomes unnecessarily cluttered.

3. Implementing the Pattern

Source code structure

For a sending function or object to call or send a message to a receiver, it must know the receiver's identity. If that is written in the source code, then the sender has a compile-time dependency on the receiver.

Often, programmers hard code the intended receiver or its concrete class. To change the receiver, the source code has to be changed and recompiled. This is slow, error-prone, blocks migration to newer technologies, and makes testing harder.

What we are looking for is a way to structure the source code so that receiver can be chosen at run time, without changing the sender's source code.

In Figure 1, using UML notation, the socket to the right of the sender indicates its *required* interface, the interface any suitable receiver must implement. The socket indicates that the sender "owns" the interface.

The ball to the left of the receivers indicates their *provided* interface, what any client of the receiver must call. The ball in the socket shows that the provided interface matches the required interface. The multiple receivers wired to the ball show that they all implement the same provided interface and can all be used there.

In some languages, the required interface is just whatever calls the sender makes. As no interface declarations are needed in such languages, there the rule is simply:
"*Don't hard-code the receiver.*"

In other languages, compile-time declarations and dependencies matter. Figure 2 shows the sender defining and owning its required interface. The receivers depend on the sender, the sender doesn't depend on any receiver. This is what we are after.

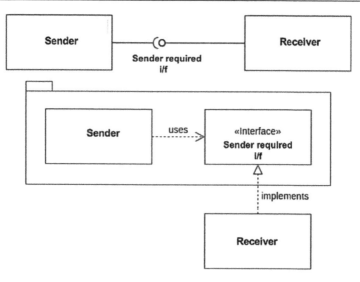

Figure 6.24. The sender owns the interface; receivers can be in different modules.

Just to show a common source-code structure that is useful in other places but does not have the property we want just now, Figure 6.25 shows the receiver defining and owning the interface. Here the sender has a compile-time dependency on the receiver. To use a different receiver we have to change the sender's source code and recompile. Not what we want here.

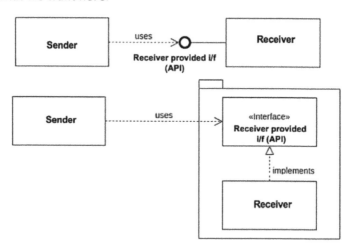

Figure 6.25. Not what we are after just now: The receiver owns the interface, the sender has a compile-time dependency on the receiver.

The configurator

At run time, something—a "configurator"—must tell the sender what receiver to use. Having a configurator is therefore part of the pattern, although the specific design of the configurator is outside the pattern.

Here are some design decisions that have to be made around the configurator:

Is the configurator hard-coded to know the sender, or is that connection made at run time?

Does the configurator drive the sender or does the sender ask the configurator?

Does the sender allow the configurator to set the receiver just once on initialization, or can the receiver be changed during execution?

These and other design decisions related to the configurator are not part of the Configurable Receiver pattern.

Run-time structure and behavior

The configurator may provide the sender with the receiver in one of two ways, making for two possible views of the pattern as implemented (Figures 6.26a and 6.26b):

* Choice 1: The configurator tells the sender what receiver to use.

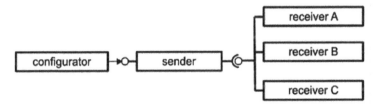

Figure 6.26a. The configurator tells the sender which receiver to use

* Choice 2: The sender asks the configurator which receiver to use.

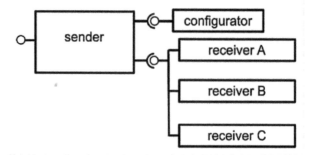

Figure 6.26b. The sender asks the configurator which receiver to use

In the first case, the configurator uses dependency injection to set the receiver. The second case uses dependency lookup: the configurator may be called a "service locator" or "broker." In effect, the first design decision for the configurator is to choose between dependency injection and dependency lookup.

You may notice a problem in the second case: How did the sender get the id of the configurator?

The relation between the sender and the configurator in this second case is exactly a copy of the sender-receiver relation that this pattern is about. Walking through "*Indications and Counterindications*," you may decide that implementing Configurable Receiver here is not worth the trouble, and you hard-code the configurator in the sender.

On the other hand, you may want to indeed repeat the pattern for the configurator. This would be appropriate for testing receivers that change dynamically during normal execution, for updating a fixed receiver in long-running systems, or when writing a library function that will use a service locator and you need the client to be able to set what locator to use.

In such cases, you would introduce a (pardon the phrase) "configurator-configurator."

To get out of the recursion here, you use the first method for the configurator-configurator—have it pass in the configurator to the sender at start-up and not change it again—and the second method for the sender-configurator pair: (Figure 5).

One implementation of Figure 6.27 is shown in sample code #4 and another in the Known Uses: Avalon framework.

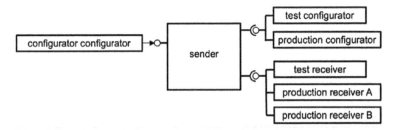

Figure 6.27. The configurator-configurator sends in a configurator to use as a service locator or broker for which receiver to use.

4. Sample Code

Here are examples creating and using a Configurable Receiver, moving from the simplest situation, using a function as the sender, to more complicated examples involving repositories. They are in different languages, to show the differences when using dynamic and statically type-checked languages:

1. A Configurable Receiver for objects, passing in the receiver at object creation time (in Ruby)

2. A Configurable Receiver for objects, passing in the receiver at object creation time (in Java)

3. A Configurable Receiver for objects, in which the configurator passes in the receiver at any time, to be used until further notice (in Java)

4. A Configurable Receiver in which the configurator is a repository and a configurator-configurator sets the configurator (in Ruby)

(1) A Configurable Receiver for objects, passing in the receiver at object creation time (in Ruby)

Here is an example of the configurator passing the receiver to the sender at object creation time. For this example, I imagine many future technologies for the tax rate repository: a test harness, a file, a database, or else direct connections to the tax office of various countries, hence needing different adapters.

For early development, I use an in-code tax rate repository with just one, fixed, tax rate.

Main is the configurator. It creates the receiver, FixedTaxRateRepository, and sends it to the sender object, the TaxCalculator, as part of the constructor.

I show Ruby code first, because as we don't have to declare the interfaces, the pattern is easier to see:

```
class TaxCalculator
  def initialize( tax_rate_repository )
    @tax_rate_repository = tax_rate_repository
  end

  def tax_cn( amount )
    amount * @tax_rate_repository.tax_rate( amount )
  end
end

class FixedTaxRateRepository
  def tax_rate( amount )
    0.15
  end
end

tax_rate_repository = FixedTaxRateRepository.new
my_calculator = TaxCalculator.new( tax_rate_repository )
puts my_calculator.tax_on( 2000 )
```

Thank you, ChatGPT.

(2) A Configurable Receiver for objects, passing in the receiver at object creation time (in Java)

Here is the same example, using Java to show the interfaces being declared.

```java
interface ForGettingTaxRates {
   double taxRate(double amount);
}

class TaxCalculator {
   private ForGettingTaxRates taxRateRepository;

   public TaxCalculator(ForGettingTaxRates taxRateRepository) {
      this.taxRateRepository = taxRateRepository;
   }

   public double taxOn(double amount) {
      return amount * taxRateRepository.taxRate( amount );
   }
}

class FixedTaxRateRepository implements ForGettingTaxRates {
   public double taxRate(double amount) {
      return 0.15;
   }
}

class Main {
   public static void main(String[] args) {
      ForGettingTaxRates taxRateRepository = new FixedTaxRateRepository();
      TaxCalculator myCalculator = new TaxCalculator( taxRateRepository );
      System.out.println( myCalculator.taxOn( 2000 ) );
   }
}
```

Thank you, ChatGPT.

(3) A Configurable Receiver for objects, in which the configurator passes in the receiver at any time, to be used until further notice (in Java)

In this example, we move the setting of the receiver into a public function that can be called at any time. This is useful when the receiver might be changed dynamically.

```java
interface ForGettingTaxRates {
   double taxRate(double amount);
}

class TaxCalculator {
   private ForGettingTaxRates taxRateRepository;

   public void setTaxRateRepository(ForGettingTaxRates taxRateRepository)
{
      this.taxRateRepository = taxRateRepository;
   }

   public double taxOn(double amount) {
      return amount * taxRateRepository.taxRate( amount );
   }
}

class FixedTaxRateRepository implements ForGettingTaxRates {
   public double taxRate(double amount) {
      return 0.15;
   }
}

class Main {
   public static void main(String[] args) {
      ForGettingTaxRates taxRateRepository = new
FixedTaxRateRepository();
      TaxCalculator myCalculator = new TaxCalculator();
      myCalculator.setTaxRateRepository( taxRateRepository );
      System.out.println(myCalculator.taxOn( 2000 ));
   }
}
```

Thank you, ChatGPT.

(4) A Configurable Receiver in which the configurator is a repository and a configurator-configurator sets the configurator (in Ruby)

The configurator-configurator example, matching Figure 5. (A second example is shown in the Avalon framework, in Known Uses.)

In Figure 6, different tax rate sources are used in different countries. The calculator asks the RateRepositoryBroker what tax rate repository to use each time. We could hard code the link from TaxCalculator to RateRepositoryBroker, but we let Main (the configurator-configurator in this case) supply RateRepositoryBroker to the TaxCalculator at the start.

This example illustrates *Dependency Injection* as Main passes the RateRepositoryBroker to TaxCalculator, and *Dependency Lookup* with TaxCalculator asking the RateRepositoryBroker each time which rate repository to use.

Choosing Ruby this time because the intention is easier to see.

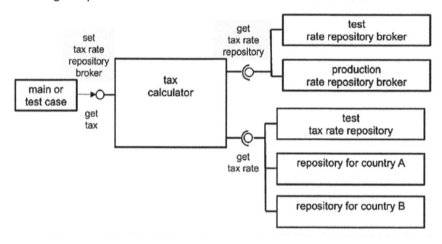

Figure 6.28. Main provides a broker to use to look up receivers.

```
class RateRepositoryBroker
  def initialize
    @tax_rate_repository_FR = TaxRateRepositoryFR.new
    @tax_rate_repository_US = TaxRateRepositoryUS.new
  end
  def repository_for( country )
    if country == "US"    return @tax_rate_repository_US
```

```
    elsif country == "FR"  return @tax_rate_repository_FR
    else  return nil
    end
  end
end

class TaxCalculator

  def initialize( repository_broker )
   @my_rate_repository_broker = repository_broker
  end

  def tax_on( country, amount )
    tax_rate_repository = @my_rate_repository_broker.repository_for(
country )
    amount * tax_rate_repository.tax_rate( amount )
  end

end


class TaxRateRepositoryFR
  def tax_rate( amount )
   0.30
  end
end

class TaxRateRepositoryUS
  def tax_rate( amount )
   0.15
  end
end

my_tax_rate_broker = RateRepositoryBroker.new
my_calculator = TaxCalculator.new( my_tax_rate_broker )
puts my_calculator.tax_rate( "FR", 2000 )
puts my_calculator.tax_rate( "US", 2000 )
```

5. Known Uses

The Spring framework

Spring supports all variants of *Configurable Receiver*. From the original article [https://docs.oracle.com/javaee/7/api/javax/inject/package-summary.html]:

This package specifies a means for obtaining objects in such a way as to maximize reusability, testability and maintainability compared to traditional approaches such as constructors, factories, and service locators (e.g., JNDI). This process, known as dependency injection, is beneficial to most nontrivial applications.

A note on vocabulary. That article says "dependency injection" includes dependency lookup. In his 2004 article Martin Fowler kept dependency lookup separate from dependency injection. [https://martinfowler.com/articles/injection.html]

The Avalon framework

The Avalon framework supports the configurator-configurator described in Figure 5, where the repository broker is not hard coded in the sender, but is passed in to the sender's constructor. From Martin Fowler [https://martinfowler.com/articles/injection.html]:

Dependency injection and a service locator aren't necessarily mutually exclusive concepts. A good example of using both together is the Avalon framework. Avalon uses a service locator, but uses injection to tell components where to find the locator.

Berin Loritsch sent me this simple version of my running example using Avalon.

```
public class MyMovieLister implements MovieLister, Serviceable {
    private MovieFinder finder;
    public void service( ServiceManager manager ) throws
ServiceException {
        finder = (MovieFinder)manager.lookup("finder");
    }
```

The Ports & Adapters pattern (Hexagonal architecture)

See [https://alistair.cockburn.us/hexagonal-architecture/]

The Ports & Adapters pattern requires all ports to be owned by the application, so they can all be connected at run time.

* Each *driving* port is published as the application's *provided* interface, making that port configurable with regard to its senders (and using the compile-time dependency structure shown in Figure 6.25).

* Each *driven* port is published as the application's *required* interface, making that port configurable with regard to its receivers (using the compile-time dependency structure shown in Figure 6.24).

Ports & Adapters does not say what form of configurator should be used. Any of the ones described in Configurable Receiver may be used.

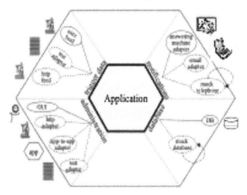

Figure 6.29. Ports & Adapters as known use of Configurable Receiver

6. Related Patterns

The Strategy pattern

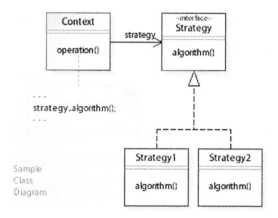

Figure 6.30: The Strategy pattern
(source: https://en.wikipedia.org/wiki/Strategy_pattern)

The Strategy pattern says that the "context" object has in its hands one of a set of possible objects that all respond to the same function call. The context object defines its required interface. Then, any of the conforming strategy objects can be used.

The Strategy pattern does not show the configurator. That is considered outside the pattern definition. Any of the configurators described in this article may be used.

Dependency Injection

From [https://en.wikipedia.org/wiki/Dependency_injection]:

dependency injection is a design pattern in which an object or function receives other objects or functions that it depends on ... Fundamentally, dependency injection consists of passing parameters to a method.

In *Dependency Injection* the configurator tells the sender what receiver to use.

Dependency Lookup

From [http://xunitpatterns.com/Dependency%20Lookup.html]:

We avoid hard-coding the names of classes on which we depend into our code because static binding severely limits our options for how the software is configured as it runs. Instead, we hard-code that name of a "component broker" that returns to us a ready to use object.

In *Dependency Lookup* the sender asks the configurator what receiver to use.

Here they say the sender contains a hard-coded reference to the broker. That is not required (see [https://springframework.guru/service-locator-pattern-in-spring/] and Known Uses: Avalon). The key phrase is "returns to us a ready-to-use object."

7. Discussion of Dependency Inversion, Injection, Lookup

Configurable Receiver makes use of all three, *dependency inversion principle, dependency injection, dependency lookup*. As these terms confuse many people, this section clarifies the relationship. Additionally, *Inversion of control* is often conflated with those three patterns, although it is unrelated.

Part of the confusion is that "dependency" refers ambiguously to a compile-time or run-time dependency. Then, "inverting" something says to do the *"not"* of some other, unnamed thing. As a consequence, dependency inversion, dependency injection, dependency lookup and inversion of control are often mixed together in incorrect ways

This discussion here is subset [https://alistaircockburn.com/Articles/Discussion-of-dependency-injection-etc]. Please refer to that for the longer discussion.

7.1. Dependency Inversion Principle (a compile-time topic)

The *Dependency Inversion Principle* refers to compile-time dependencies between two elements. "Inversion" in the name refers to the formerly dominant hierarchical decomposition techniques in which abstract decisions were higher up in the hierarchy and depended on the concrete implementations that were lower down. The principle says: "Do the opposite of that."

Element A has a *compile-time* dependency on element B if it needs B to be present for its (A's) compilation. If B's implementation changes, A has to be recompiled.

The dependency inversion principle says:

The Dependency Inversion Principle:

> A. HIGH LEVEL MODULES SHOULD NOT DEPEND UPON LOW LEVEL MODULES. BOTH SHOULD DEPEND UPON ABSTRACTIONS.

> B. ABSTRACTIONS SHOULD NOT DEPEND UPON DETAILS. DETAILS SHOULD DEPEND UPON ABSTRACTIONS.

https://web.archive.org/web/20110714224327/http://www.objectmentor.
com/resources/articles/dip.pdf,
https://en.wikipedia.org/wiki/Dependency_inversion_principle

From Bob Martin's original article:

One might question why I use the word "inversion." Frankly, it is
because more traditional software development methods, such as
Structured Analysis and Design, tend to create software structures in
which high level modules depend upon low level modules, and in which
abstractions depend upon details. Indeed, one of the goals of these
methods is to define the subprogram hierarchy that describes how the
high level modules make calls to the low level modules.

Note here the date of the article: 1996. People were still predominantly
using structured analysis and structured design. In those, one started
with an abstract statement of policy at a higher level in the hierarchy
and detailed that down to some specific implementation at a lower level
in the hierarchy. "Higher" and "lower" levels made sense to talk about,
and "more abstract" and "less abstract" similarly.

This changed with OO languages. As there is no hierarchical
decomposition, there is no obvious "higher" and "lower" level in an OO
design. What remain is the thought that there is a policy decision, like
"notify people when the situation changes", and various execution
possibilities, like telephones, pagers, emails, etc. Although it is not as
obvious as it was before, we can apply the thought, "There are various
ways to do that" to get to what Bob Martin refers to as "lower level."

Thus, if

there are various ways to do that

then apply the design idea.

In fact, you will apply the Configurable Receiver pattern, as described
later: Define the policy object's required interface, add an instance
variable to hold the receiver at run time, design the configurator to
provide the receiver to use at run time, and go.

In his example of a button telling a lamp to turn on and off, is a button
higher-level than a lamp? Hardly. Is the button setting a policy decision
that lamps implement? Not really. Here, he considers the button being
used for many devices, such as a hot tub or a radio, so "there are

various things to turn on and off" becomes the direction of the principle.

Leaving aside higher and lower levels, if we want the button to control various things, then we might ignore the phrase "dependency inversion", but focus on the key recommendation: "both depend upon abstractions."

Also, programming language matters. Bob Martin writes about C++:

The definition of a class, in the .h module, contains declarations of all the member functions and member variables of the class. This information goes beyond simple interface. All the utility functions and private variables needed by the class are also declared in the .h module.

For that reason, he uses abstract classes with no implementation details. Languages like Java, have interfaces which are the equivalent. And of course, dynamic languages need none of this, since they don't declare interfaces, so the entire matter is simply: Don't hard-code the receiver class.

Should, in a different situation, we need the lamp to be controlled by other things, like a dimmer switch, or voice, or signals from external devices, it becomes even more unclear which is higher level, and in particular, who should own which interface.

In this case, the design question is: Who owns the interface definition?

When working in a large project, one solution is to put the interface definition in a separate module, referenced by two different teams, and the interface module becomes the shared agreement of the interface between the teams.

In May, 2023, I asked Bob Martin to comment on the above text. He replied:

> Nowadays I define level the way Page-Jones defined it so long ago: distance from IO.

Relating the dependency inversion principle to the Configurable Receiver pattern, the dependency inversion principle has the sender declaring a *required* interface so that different receivers can be used with the minimal amount of recompilation. The dependency inversion principle mentions the reasons to choose this design and describes the required interface, but does not mention the configurator.

7.2. Dependency Injection (a run-time topic))

From [https://en.wikipedia.org/wiki/Dependency_injection]:

dependency injection is a design pattern in which an object or function receives other objects or functions that it depends on ... Fundamentally, dependency injection consists of passing parameters to a method.

Element A has a *run-time* dependency on element B if it needs B to be present at run time to receive a call from A. If B is deleted before A calls it, A's call fails.

In this case, there is a third element, C, which knows about B and passes B as a argument to A, whether in A's constructor or through some other interface. Once A has that information, A has a run-time dependency on B; B had better not get deleted before A calls on it.

Dependency Injection is a way of saying *how* A comes to know of B: C tells A.
It says nothing about what A does with B afterwards.

7.3. Dependency Lookup (a run-time topic)

Dependency Lookup is the other way for element A to get B's identity at run time:
A asks some third party C for that information.

From [http://xunitpatterns.com/Dependency%20Lookup.html]:

... a "component broker" that returns to us a ready to use object.

Leaving aside the unnecessary writing in that entry about hard coding things, this pattern says that there is a third element C that knows which B to use at that moment.
A asks C for the information as needed.

In the text, they suggest that the sender contains a hard-coded reference to the broker. This is not necessary. A may come to know of C in any of the three ways: hard-coded, dependency injection, or dependency lookup.

In general, there are two ways for A to learn of B, when it is not hard-coded:

A asks C about B (dependency lookup)

C tells A about B (dependency injection)

In terms of the Configurable Receiver pattern, C is the "configurator" in both cases. It has the magical information of which B A needs to use.

Common to the *Dependency Injection* and *Dependency Lookup* is that they describe only *how* A obtains the B's identity. The patterns say nothing about what A does with it afterwards. This is relevant when analyzing *Inversion of Control*.

7.4. Inversion of Control (a run-time topic)

Inversion of Control is a run-time concept that is unrelated to any of the patterns described so far. It is often misrepresented. Even the Wikipedia entry had to be updated to correct the errors previously there [https://en.wikipedia.org/wiki/Inversion_of_control].

This idea was first publicized in a 1985 paper describing the Mesa system, using the phrase "Hollywood's Law" [https://digibarn.com/friends/curbow/star/XDEPaper.pdf]:

Don't call us, we'll call you (Hollywood's Law). A tool should arrange for Tajo to notify it when the user wishes to communicate some event to the tool, rather than adopt an "ask the user for a command and execute it" model

"Inversion of control" was used in passing in the 1988 paper, "Designing Reusable Classes" by Ralph Johnson and Brian Foote

One important characteristic of a framework is that the methods defined by the user to tailor the framework will often be called from within the framework itself, rather than from the user's application code. The framework often plays the role of the main program in coordinating and sequencing application activity. This inversion of control gives frameworks the power to serve as extensible skeletons. The methods supplied by the user tailor the generic algorithms defined in the framework for a particular application.

Note here that what they are describing has nothing in common with what we have been talking about so far in terms of dependency inversion, injection or lookup. It is a totally unrelated concept.

In *Inversion of Control*, element A registers interest in a topic with element B, or the injection framework does that registration. Then when B has something of interest for element A, B calls or sends a message to A.

Note this is always a two-step process:

1. A registers or gets registered with B to set up a callback location.

2. When B detects a relevant event, it calls back to that callback location.

A suitable alternative word would be "callback."

The "inversion" mentioned here is a reference to a "normal" call sequence, where A calls B to render a service, and A is in control of the call timing.

In the new situation, once B has A's id, B takes control of the timing, and calls A when something important happens. Hence, "inversion of control."

Inversion of control is a characteristic of frameworks, as opposed to libraries.

When using library element B, A calls B to perform some task.

When using framework element B, B calls element A for the specialized behavior needed to make the framework fit that situation.

This mechanism is widely used with UI frameworks, event systems, and ASP.NET. In each, the framework "wakes up" our object to handle some event.

Here is how .NET uses inversion of control (from "Dependency Injection in .NET", Mark Seemann):

The term Inversion of Control (IoC) originally meant any sort of programming style where an overall framework or runtime controlled the program flow. According to that definition, most software developed on the .NET Framework uses IoC.

When you write an ASP.NET application, you hook into the ASP.NET page life cycle, but you aren't in control-ASP.NET is.

When you write a WCF service, you implement interfaces decorated with attributes.

You may be writing the service code, but ultimately, you aren't in control- WCF is.

These days, we're so used to working with frameworks that we don't consider this to be special, but it's a different model from being in full control of your code.

This can still happen for a .NET application most notably for command-line executables. As soon as Main is invoked, your code is in full control. It controls program flow, life-time, everything. No special events are being raised and no overridden members are being invoked.

I hope you see his clear description of "normal" verses "inverted" control. If you write Main, you are in "normal" control. If you write an ASP.NET application, you do the two steps mentioned:

First, hook into the ASP.NET page life cycle.

Then, ASP.NET takes control and calls your code when events warrant it.

"Normal" control and "inversion of control" can be used in alternation. I like to think of inversion of control as setting a callback, where the callback code just continues the conversation between A and B, filling in some information B needs.

For tracing the behavior of A and B in inversion of control, a nice, simple example to walk through is the Observer pattern. In this example, the observer is A and the subject is B.
[https://en.wikipedia.org/wiki/Observer_pattern].

Notice in the following that there is no element C that has to introduce them to each other. How A comes to know about B is not part of the *Inversion of Control* pattern.

In Figure 6.31, we first see each observer (element A) attaching itself to the subject (B), "normal control".." Later, (B) calls each (A) back to say that something has changed. In the third step, the observer (A) calls the subject (B) in "normal control" again to ask for some specific information.

Only the step in which B calls back to A is the "inversion of control" we are referring to. What makes the subject calling the observer an "inversion of control" is the observer (A) sitting idle with respect to the subject (B) until something of interest happens and the subject takes the initiative to call the observer.

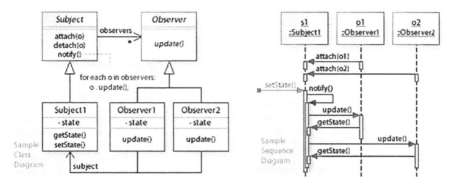

Figure 6.31. The Observer pattern (source: https://en.wikipedia.org/wiki/Observer_pattern)

Here is the example of *Inversion of Control* from Wikipedia. [https://en.wikipedia.org/wiki/Inversion_of_control]

A web application registers the endpoints it listens on with a web application framework, and then lets control pass to the framework. For instance, this example code for an Asp.NetCore web application creates an web application host, registers an endpoint, and then passes control to the framework:

```
var builder = WebApplication.CreateBuilder(args);
var app = builder.Build();
app.MapGet("/", () => "Hello World!");
app.Run();
```

Don't confuse *Inversion of Control* with *Dependency Injection* or *Dependency Lookup*, they have nothing to do with each other.

Dependency Injection and *Dependency Lookup* talk about *how* element A comes to know of element B, namely via some element C. A will then call or send a message to B in the usual way, not using inversion of control. A controls the timing of the call.

Inversion of control talks about who is in control of the timing of their interaction: If A is in control, then it's a "normal control" situation, if B is in control of the timing, then it is an "inversion of control" situation. There is no element C in the picture.

A can come to be registered with B in any manner: hardcoded, dependency injection, dependency lookup or injection framework.

7.5. Relating them all

I found it useful to put into tables the different issues they are each dealing with. Some are compile-time while others are run-time. Here are the tables:

	Compile time	Run time
Dependency Inversion Principle (DIP)	✓	
Dependency Injection (DI)		✓
Dependency Lookup (DL)		✓
Configurable Receiver (CR)	✓	✓
Inversion of Control (IoC)		✓

At Run Time:	A controls call timing	B controls call timing
An element C informs A of B	DI, DL, CR	
A comes to know B, but B doesn't need to know A	DI, DL, CR	
A & B know each other		IoC

The "dependency" in *Dependency Inversion Principle* refers to compile-time dependency. All the others are run-time topics. *Configurable Receiver* covers both.

The second table shows three issues in play at run time.

In *Dependency Injection, Dependency Lookup, Configurable Receiver*, there must be a third element C that informs A about B. This is not required in *Inversion of Control*.

In *Dependency Injection, Dependency Lookup, Configurable Receiver*, A calls B whenever it wants, B does not call back. In *Inversion of Control*, B calls A back when it wants. That call is the "inversion of control."

In all cases, A has to know B in order to make the first call. But B also has to know of A in order to make the callback in *Inversion of Control*. That makes it different: both A and B have to know the other.

In short:

* *Dependency Inversion Principle* is a compile-time recommendation on how to structure the source code so that receivers can be set at run time without having to recompile the sender:
  → In the source code, make the sender dependent on an interface that gets implemented by the allowed receivers.

* Dependency Injection says how a sender comes to know of a receiver at run time:
  → A configurator tells the sender what receiver to use.
  How they interact after that is outside the pattern.

* Dependency Lookup says how a sender comes to know of a receiver at run time:
  → The sender asks a configurator what receiver to use.
  How they interact after that is outside the pattern.

* Configurable Receiver covers both compile-time and run-time issues.
  → At compile time, the sender defines and owns a required interface that every receiver must implement. (Dependency Inversion Principle)
  → At run time, the sender either asks or is told by a configurator what receiver to use (Dependency Injection or Dependency Lookup).
  How they interact after that is outside the pattern.

* Inversion of Control is about who controls the timing of the interactions:
  → Element A calls element B using "normal control" to set up a callback method.
  → Some time later, element B calls element A (an "inversion of control" call) to tell it or ask it something.
  How A and B come to know each other is outside the pattern.

8. Final thoughts on the writing and the naming of the pattern

There is a time when what one is doing so new that the obvious way to describe it is as "not the mainstream thing." Over time, we find a term for what-it-is instead of what-it-isn't and the old term drops out of use.

* *"Horseless carriages":* Early cars were called "horseless carriages." That became irrelevant once cars took over the road, and the term was dropped. Even "auto-mobile" was once hyphenated, as an attempt to distinguish it. "Car" was originally written "motor car." And so on.

* *"Inversion":* "Inversion" is a reference to a previous something, meaning "not that." Except, it even doesn't say what it is not. For this reason, I avoid "inversion."

  Notes: In the Mesa paper, they stated, "Don't call us, we'll call you", with a slight indication of what had once been normal but wasn't being used, then focusing on what they *do* use. Johnson and Foote wrote "inversion of control" only as a passing phrase, not as a principle or a pattern name.

* *"Dependency":* Does "dependency" refer to compile-time or run-time dependency? Compile-time dependency is important, as it affects build times. Run-time dependency is important if lifetimes are the worry: we worry that A will call B but B might get deleted before that. But which one is usually not stated.

  Even at run time, we are not passing in a "dependency", we are passing in an actual object.

Thus, I avoid the terms "dependency" and "inversion" to the extent possible.

* *"Configurable Receiver":* Daniel Terhorst-North finally noticed the thing we are actually working on: the receiver, that which should receive a future message. Hence the constructive name: *Configurable Receiver*.

Hopefully saying you will "use a Configurable Receiver" is clear. Your colleague might ask "Why?" and "How?" and "Is it worth it?" and a fruitful dialog follows.

Best wishes managing your dependencies :).

With many thanks to Juan Manuel Garrido de Paz, Chris Carroll, Valentia Cupać, and Martin Fowler for their close reading of the pattern and their detailed improvements.

Chapter 7:
Summary

7.1. The pattern in its shortest form

The official name: *Ports & Adapters*

The nickname: *Hexagonal Architecture*

Thumbnail:

Create your application to work without either a UI or a database so you can run automated regression-tests against it, change connected technologies, protect it from leaks between business logic and technologies, work when the database becomes unavailable, and link applications together without any user involvement.

Why:

Test the system's functions completely with test drivers and test doubles.

Programming leaks—either business logic leaking into the technologies, or technology dependencies leaking into the business core—can be caught immediately.

Secondary actors can be changed easily, even dynamically.

App developers can continue to develop using test doubles when production repositories are unavailable.

A sample drawing, with test and production connections:

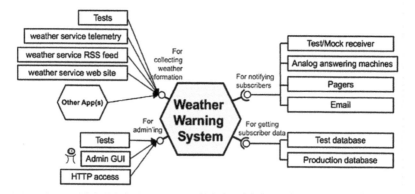

Figure 7.1. A Sample of the pattern in action

7.2. The sample code to copy

All the pages in this book only serve to help you replicate this code snippet in your larger system.

This Java code shows the interface definitions explicitly:

```java
interface ForCalculatingTaxes {
   double taxOn(double amount);
}
```

```java
interface ForGettingTaxRates {
   double taxRate(double amount);
}
```

```java
class TaxCalculator implements ForCalculatingTaxes {
   private ForGettingTaxRates taxRateRepository;
   public TaxCalculator(ForGettingTaxRates taxRateRepository) {
      this.taxRateRepository = taxRateRepository;
   }
   public double taxOn(double amount) {
      return amount *  taxRateRepository. taxRate( amount );
   }
}
```

```java
class FixedTaxRateRepository
      implements ForGettingTaxRates {
   public double taxRate(double amount) {
      return 0.15;
   }
}
```

```java
class Main {
   public static void main(String[] args) {
      ForGettingTaxRates taxRateRepository = new
                                    FixedTaxRateRepository();
      ForCalculatingTaxes myCalculator = new TaxCalculator(
                                    taxRateRepository );
      System.out.println( myCalculator.taxOn( 100 ) );
   }
```

The Ruby code that follows shows how dynamic languages arrange the same system with no interface definitions.

```ruby
class TaxCalculator
  def initialize( tax_rate_repository )
    @tax_rate_repository = tax_rate_repository
  end

  def tax_on( amount )
    amount * @tax_rate_repository.tax_rate( amount )
  end
end
```

```ruby
class FixedTaxRateRepository
  def tax_rate( amount )
    0.15
  end
end
```

```ruby
tax_rate_repository = FixedTaxRateRepository.new
my_calculator = TaxCalculator.new( tax_rate_repository )
puts my_calculator.tax_rate( 100 )
```

It took a lot of words to break down how that little bit of code is constructed, why it is done that way, and how to make it work in your setting. Copy that code into your workspace and change and grow it from there.

7.3. The costs and benefits of this pattern

Juan summarized the costs and benefits of Ports & Adapters:

Benefits:

1. Ports & Adapters improves testing by driving the app with test cases and plugging-in test-doubles at driven ports. This improvement manifests in several ways:

   * Business logic tests are fast, since they run in-memory.

   * The different components of the system (app and adapters) can be tested in isolation from each other, and integrated later.

   * When changing the source code of the application for whatever reason (a new feature, bug fixes, etc), already-completed tests can be used as regression tests. This allows you to check whether the change made introduces a non-desired behavior in the already existing functionality, as well as to check any logic leakage between the app and the outside world.

2. Methodologies like TDD (Test Driven Development) and BDD (Behavior Driven Development) are easier to apply. This doesn't mean that Ports & Adapters prescribes the use of these methodologies. You could use an inside-out methodology as well, programming the whole app first and testing afterward.

3. Ports & Adapters improves maintainability. Maintainable systems are those that are easy to modify. Ports & Adapters increases maintainability by providing a separation of concerns and business logic decoupling, which makes it easier to locate the code you want to modify.

4. Application maintainability is a long-term concept related to technical debt. The more maintainability, the less technical debt. So, Ports & Adapters reduces the technical debt.

5. Flexibility: The Ports & Adapters mechanism makes it easier to swap technologies and to add new ones.

6. The application is immune to technological evolution, because technologies can be updated without changing the application.

7. Business logic can be developed without needing to know which technologies will be used, which allows for the delaying of technological decisions.

Costs:

1. The structure, start-up process and building of the whole system is more complex than in other architectures, such as the classic three-layered architecture.

2. Ports & Adapters introduces one more level of indirection on the driven side, since adapters must translate required interfaces into specific interfaces of the different technologies.

3. It might introduce additional mappers that map entities of the domain model into entities of the persistence model, and vice-versa.

4. Learning this architecture is hard. It requires experience and is difficult for novice programmers.

5. The starting of a new project takes more time than with other architectures, so Ports & Adapters may be best suited for medium-to-large projects.

Balancing the Costs and the Benefits:

People who have never been hurt by changing technology, changing interfaces, business logic leaking out, external technology details leaking in, or having to recompile the system to switch between testing and production, are more likely to say that the costs look too high to be worth implementing.

It's not until things go wrong, and people suffer during project development, that they change their minds and decide that adding a few interfaces and instance variables is worth the trouble.

For the two of us, this is now our default way of building applications or systems. It would take special circumstances, like writing a one-off program, for us not to use it.

7.4. Why the name "Hexagonal" Architecture?

Already discussed in section 1.3, but some people like to jump to the end:

The name "Hexagonal Architecture" was a placeholder name I (Alistair) came up with years before I understood what the sides of the hexagon stood for. I just knew they had to be there. It is not really a good pattern name since he number six has no particular meaning. You might have three, five, or any number of ports, not six. Additionally, a hexagon is just a geometric shape. It doesn't show up anywhere in your software.

So why the name, and why change it to the more descriptive *Ports & Adapters*? The best answer is what I wrote in the RSS feed from 2005, when I finally worked out what the facets meant:

> *Somewhere in the mid-90s I started drawing a symmetric architecture in which the database is considered not at the "bottom of the stack", but fully outside the application, just as we recommend doing with the user interface.*
>
> *To break up perceptions about top and bottom and left and right, I drew it with a hexagonal shape, and came up with the rather lame name HexagonalArchitecture --- simply because I could not identify think of what the "hexagon" meant, but knew it had to have facets, and no number smaller than 5 made visual sense (and pentagons are harder to draw than hexagons).*
>
> *Finally just worked out what the drawing meant and realized this picture or architecture should be called Ports and Adapters (think operating system or hi-fi ports, and Design Pattern "adapters").*
> *--*
> *https://web.archive.org/web/20060318201137/http:/alistair.cockburn.us/rss.rdf (time stamp: 2005 07 15 13:01 MST)*

"Hexagonal Architecture" has served well as a hook to the pattern. It's easy to remember and generates conversation. However, in this book we want to be correct: The name of the pattern is "Ports & Adapters", because there really are ports, and there really are adapters, and your architecture will show them.

The main problem with the terms Hexagonal Architecture is that it leads people to just draw hexagons all over the place, citing "hexagons", without ever implementing the actual Ports & Adapters architecture.

Therefore, whenever you get into a technical discussion, drop the word "hexagon", and say "ports" instead. We believe that will make your architecture better and clear up many misunderstandings.

Fin

I want to thank Christopher Hayes-Kossmann for copy-editing the preview edition. Hemal Varambhia make a spectacular gift proofing this updated edition with his eagle eyes. Hemal, Simone Giusso, Rob Jarratt, Ricardo Guzmán Velasco, Nicky Ramone, Chris Carroll, and Eleonora Ciceri did some really detailed reading and provided great feedback.

It is strange that I have been describing this pattern for 30 years. It is a really simple architecture to implement, and yet we are still discovering relationships to other people's work and other patterns. As someone commented, the code is much simpler than the descriptions of the pattern. It is for that reason that we show the code in the first and last sections of the book.

And finally, for me, Alistair, I feel like I lost half of my Hexagonal brain with the passing of Juan Manuel Garrido de Paz. He was the person I always wrote to when someone posed a new question or I had a doubt about a piece of code. His knowledge was encyclopedic, his method analytical. We debated incessantly until we agreed on an answer that satisfied us both.

Here is his favorite image he sent me during those discussions:

R.I.P. Juan Manuel Garrido de Paz. Thank you.

About the Authors

Dr. Alistair Cockburn (pronounced CO-BURN), known for his wild hair photo on LinkedIn, was named as one of the "42 Greatest Software Professionals of All Times" in 2020, as a world expert on object-oriented development, software architecture, project management, use cases and agile development. Since 2015 he has

been working on expanding agile to cover every kind of initiative, including social impact project, governments, and families. For his latest work, see https://alistaircockburn.com/.

Juan Manuel Garrido de Paz (August 3, 1970 - April 18, 2024) won his Bachelor in Software Engineering at the Polytechnic University of Madrid. He became the world's other leading authority on the Ports & Adapters pattern by probing and interacting with Dr. Alistair Cockburn over years. A senior developer for the government of Andalucía, his two passions were Hexagonal Architecture and Recreativo de Huelva Football Club. Sadly, Juan passed away just weeks before this book went to print. This book is dedicated to him and his life.

www.ingramcontent.com/pod-product-compliance
Lightning Source LLC
LaVergne TN
LVHW061956050326
832903LV00039B/4832